Gender: Themes and Issues

About the Author

Dr. Jyoti Prasad Saikia is currently Professor in the Department of Sociology, Dibrugarh University, Assam. He is working in the field of Gender studies and social pathology. He has written and edited a number of books. Among these, 'Youth and Career Aspiration', 'Problems of Education in Rural Women', 'Rendering Gender,' 'Gender Trouble: A Study in North-East India,' 'Gender & Health : A Sociological Insight,' 'Contemporary Indian Society', 'Flash from North-East India' are significant. Apart from these, he has written more than thirty text books on sociology.

GENDER
THEMES AND ISSUES

Revised and Enlarged Edition

Jyoti Prasad Saikia
Department of Sociology
Dibrugarh University
Dibrugarh, Assam

CONCEPT PUBLISHING COMPANY PVT. LTD.
NEW DELHI-110059

ISBN-13: 978-93-5125-283-2 (HB)
ISBN-13: 978-93-5125-284-9 (PB)

Revised & Enlarged Edition 2017

Published and Printed by

Concept Since 1974

Concept Publishing Company Pvt. Ltd.
A/15-16, Commercial Block, Mohan Garden,
New Delhi-110059 (INDIA)
T : 011 25351460, 011 25351794
E : publishing@conceptpub.com; *W* : www.conceptpub.com

Cataloging in Publication Data--Courtesy: D.K. Agencies (P) Ltd. <docinfo@dkagencies.com>

Saikia, Jyoti Prasad, author.
Gender : themes and issues / Jyoti Prasad Saikia. -- Revised and enlarged edition.
pages cm
Includes bibliographical references and index.
ISBN 9789351252832 (HB)
ISBN 9789351252849 (PB)

1. Sex discrimination against women—India. 2. Sex discrimination against women. 3. Women—Crimes against—India. 4. Women—Crimes against. 5. Women—India—Social conditions. 6. Women—Social conditions. I. Title.

HQ1237.5.I4S25 2017 DDC 305.420954 23

Dedicated to my respected teacher
Prof. B. N. Borthakur
&
Prof. Maqitul Hussain
who taught me to think and feel about
Gender Studies

Foreword

I consider it a great privilege when I was requested by Dr. Jyoti Prasad Saikia to write the foreword for his book "Gender: Themes and Issues" mainly for two reasons — his continuous efforts, as I know from my long association with him, to delve deep into sociological interpretations of a social phenomenon and his untiring interest in contemporary new social issues.

His book addresses such an area of investigation which remained almost dormant throughout the intellectual domain of late twentieth century. There is no doubt a number of worthwhile publications had already appeared since 1970s. But Jyoti's book is certainly not a mere casual addition to the list of publications on the topic related to 'Gender' which had already cut across several academic disciplines like sociology, economics, politics, linguistics, history, psychology and law because his meticulous presentations in this book will attract attention from different intellectual corners due to its certain unique features.

The book is sub-divided into several major chapters carefully initiating the subject and its conceptual issues followed by theories available in sociological literature to understand this area of gender in a changing global society. Simple description of Anthropological, Biological and Ethological orientations of 'gender' or 'sex' becomes an offbeat interpretation of human existence in a growing world of Globalization *vis-à-vis* multi-culturalization. Jyoti has driven the point that the issue of 'gender' should be addressed sociologically and it definitely penetrates through the nuances of pre-post-modernist sociologists like Peter Berger and post-modern thinkers like Foucault or Lyotard. Mead Berger and Cooley and Goffman placed the issue of 'self' or 'identity' as the prime mover in understanding 'gender-role' or 'sex-role' in a specified society. In Jyoti's analysis one finds the echoes of Berger:

> *"The self is a reflected entity, reflecting the attitudes first taken by significant other forward it: the individual becomes what he is addressed as by his significant other. That is not a one sided mechanistic process. It entails a dialectic between objectivity assigned and subjectivity appropriated identity".* (P. Berger, *'Modern Identity — Crisis and Continuity',* Washington D.C. Smithsonian Institute, 1970)

The gender issue, Jyoti rightly pointed out, is intermixed with sex-role stereotyping in our societies due to the interpretation of masculinity and femininity. The entering of the theoretical debates at this juncture of his book provides ample opportunities to his readers to see the detailed contours of individual socialization and socio-economic-political divides. It is indeed very refreshing.

Jyoti places 'The Gender' like the post-modernists viz. Derrida (Philosophers can work only at the 'margins' of reality — *Margins of Reality,* Chicago University, 1983) or Jean Gebrse (Periphery must be brought to the centre and now the centre is everywhere and anywhere in the society, *The Everpresent Origin,* Ohio University, 1985, p. 544).

Other influences of post-modernists on Jyoti's writings will be found by his reader of this book. The issues of Homosexuals, Lesbians and other so-called peripheral social groups have already made inroads into the traditionally defined content of sexual stereotyping not only in the Western society, but also in our own society, i.e. India or Assam to be specific. The legislations related to gender crimes as delineated by the author allows any reader of his book to engage in self-analysis. Harassment of women in different social institutions is no longer a private matter of few individuals, but a social problem as C.W. Mills six decades ago beautifully identified.

Jyoti has not forgotten the classical sociologists who also provided certain insights into the gender issues. He has brought the topic out of the closet squeezed so long in the shadowy corner of publications. Another commendable task accomplished by Jyoti is to touch certain new yet extremely important and sensitive issues in the field of gender studies such as gendering caste, gendered bodies, gender budgeting, Ecofeminism etc.

Overall, it can be said that he has provided a significant analysis of 'gender' and related issues and allows his readers to feel the masterly strokes of a scholar. This unputdownable book of Dr. Jyoti Prasad Saikia should be read by interested students and intellectuals who like to say—"Hai! Here is a book I have been looking for...! It is a whip of fresh air!!"

Maqitul Hussain

Former Professor, Department of Sociology,
Dibrugarh University
&
Head, Department of Sociology,
Rajiv Gandhi Central University,
Itanagar, Arunachal Pradesh

Preface to the Revised Edition

Sociology of Gender, in recent times, has emerged as one of the most leading branches of Sociology. The centrality of gender in today's sociological discourse has been caused by its now recognized relevance to reality of varied social phenomena among many other things. Thus, the concept of gender developed under the parameters of sociological discourse influences not only the sociologists and other academicians of related social sciences, but also economists, political scientists and even the politicians and policy-makers. This influence is clearly visible in the efforts being made by humanitarian and political bodies such as UN and governments at both national and international levels to make gender an essential part of their policies to develop and empower. As the gender discourse is capable of including under its arms the physiological, psychological, social and cultural differences between men and women and exposing the relationship between them as never seen or understood before, gender has become much more than just a concept to explain the differences and inequalities between men and women. The discourse on gender has developed the concept of gender into a perspective which can be used to explore and understand complex social phenomena in a novel and unique way. Thus, study of gender sociology has the potential to play a vital role in creating awareness of social discrimination and uprooting social evils that exist in our society. This is why sociology of gender has received its vitality within the sociological discourse and beyond. And the same stands as the cause behind writing of this book. Here, I have made an attempt to include some selected topics related to gender sociology along with their critical theoretical interpretations. I have also included and have attempted to analyze some of the burning issues of today, particularly in the Indian context such as witch hunting. I have added my own views regarding these issues which I have developed through my experiences in both the academic and non-academic fields. If this book meets the needs of time, I shall feel myself rewarded and succeeded.

Jyoti Prasad Saika

Preface to the First Edition

Sociology of Gender is now one of the most leading branches of sociology. The study of Gender in Sociology influences the present day scholars and academics in a very unique way. Sociological interpretation of Gender is very significant and interesting for each and every aspect in social sciences. It concerns the psychological, social and cultural differences between males and females. Making a clear distinction between sex and gender from sociological understanding, it is considered that gender is socially constructed concept. So, gender refers to cultural and social explanation that turns sexual difference rather than biological distinction from sociology. This branch of sociology may play a vital role creating awareness of social discrimination and also help in uprooting social evils that has still existed in our Indian society. If my work meets the needs of time, I shall feel myself rewarded and succeeded.

In this small book, I have made an effort to discuss some selected issues of gender along with the theoretical interpretation. In this regard, it can be considered as experiences which have been gathered through my works in both academic and non-academic fields.

I am offering my sincere regards and gratitude to Prof. Maqitul Hussain and Prof. B.N. Borthakur who provided their full guidance, encouragement and co-operation in attaining my goal. I will always remain grateful to them. I am also thankful to my wife Mrs. Mitali Gogoi for her whole hearted co-operation and assistance to complete this book. I must also mention the inspiration that the heart warming smile of my son Bristiborna (Raag) provided me. I am also thankful to my sister Priyanku Priya Saikia, elder brother Charu Prasad Saikia, Prasanta Kumar Chutia, Mridul Phukan who offered their helping hands to write the book in timeframe. I am also thankful to my Research Scholar Hriday Ranjan Kalita for his patience and the pain he took while helping me to prepare this revised edition.

My junior colleagues Mr. Partha Pratim Borah and Annanya Gogoi also deserve my thanks for their co-operation to write a book on gender. I owe an immense debt to my late father Probin Kr. Chutia and mother Labanya Chutia for taking pains during my student life, without which I would not have been able to undertake this educative venture. I would like to convey my thanks to Parvez Hussain, Dhrubajyoti Konwar and Rajib Ali for preparation of this script successfully.

Last but not the least; I take pleasure to express my heartiest thanks to Mr. Biswajit Saikia and Ranjit Saikia of Bidyabhawan, for undertaking all the responsibilities of publishing this small book. I shall remain ever indebted to them.

Dibrugarh University, **Jyoti Prasad Saikia**
Dibrugarh, Assam

Acknowledgements

I am offering my sincere regards and gratitude to Prof. Maqitul Hussain and Prof. B.N. Borthakur who bestowed their guidance and encouragement upon me. I will always remain grateful to them. I am also thankful to my wife Mrs. Mitali Gogoi for her whole hearted co-operation and assistance in completing this book. I must also mention the inspiration that the heart warming smile of my son Bristiborna (Raag) provided me. I am also thankful to my sister Priyanku Priya Saikia, elder brother Charu Prasad Saikia, Ranjit Saikia, Makhan Saikia, Hemanta Kumar Hazarika, Prasanta Kumar Chutia, Mridul Phukan who offered their helping hands to write the book in time. I am also thankful to my Research Scholar Hriday Ranjan Kalita for his valuable help in preparing this revised edition. The faculty members of the department also deserve my thanks for their co-operation to write a book on gender. I owe an immense debt to my late father Probin Kr. Chutia and mother Labanya Chutia for taking pains during my student life, without which I would not have been able to undertake this academic endeavour. I would like to convey my thanks to Parvez Hussain for preparation of this script successfully. Last but not the least; I take pleasure to express my heartiest thanks to the Concept Publishing Company Pvt. Ltd., for undertaking the publication of this book. I shall remain ever indebted to them.

Dibrugarh University,
Dibrugarh, Assam

Jyoti Prasad Saikia

Contents

1
Sociology of Gender: An Introduction

In recent years, Gender studies have attracted the attention of a considerable number of Social Scientists. Even now it has expanded the boundaries of Sociology and also attracted the attention of various scholars around the world. In this regard, it can be considered as an integral part of all human experiences. Though, sociologists develop the paradigm as well as sociological theories on gender issue, several new developments emerged. Social scientists have led to a variety of viewpoints and perspectives. It is also true, some of the rigorous social scientists and critics have raised the question—Why the word 'gender' is used instead of "women"? A section of them prefer gender studies rather than women studies. Therefore, sociologists also advocate using of the term 'Sociology of Gender' instead of 'Sociology of Women'. But it is not an ultimate consensus of all sociologists that "Women's studies have to be understood in the context of the genesis of women's movement and its location within it. Established Indian women scholars and activists emphasize the difference between women's studies and gender studies. They refrain from using gender because it diverts the focus from the women to gender issues and the use of gender as a conceptual category along with class, race, ethnicity and caste has expanded the horizon of sociology."[1] Keeping with this view, I am always in a very combating position; whether it should be called as sociology of gender or Sociology of women. But I, being a student of sociology, wish take privilege to prefer 'Sociology of Gender'. Gender sociology or sociology of gender is now established as one of the most important branches of sociology. Though the terms 'gender studies' and 'women studies' are being used interchangeably to mean the new areas of study relating to the question of women, patriarchy and gender discourse and both the terms have legitimately got acceptance as emerging discipline, a critical perspective may help to discern finer differences in between the two terms. Emergence of new areas of the study on the marginal groups such as gay, lesbian, transgender have widen the scope of the discipline—gender studies emphasizes its focus on women's questions and the issues emerging out of the feminist movement. In the first part of the 1960, the emergence of the gender studies was associated with the political movement and practice of feminism. But in course of time, women scholars started to challenge the discrimination more vocally in different spheres. They began to feel that this discrimination makes them unequal to men not only in domestic responsibilities, but also in education, economy, polity, religion etc. Keeping this view in the mind women studies activists and scholars strived to rectify this pliable situation. This effort was made by providing proper information and analysis regarding the lives of women; therefore, that they could be used to take initiative for social changes that would end gender inequality. In this way, a serious question always exists in my mind: How can men and women be equal? From the very beginning when human beings were evolved, both men and women have been playing different roles according to their own feasibility, capacity, and mental growth. Men were considered to be suited to do work outside the house and women were seen as perfect home makers. Both men and women possess different hormones, for which, they are different not only physically, but also emotionally and intellectually. But this argument is more and more complicated and no resolution seems to be in sight Gender Studies activities, scholars and feminist writers not to accept this complicated argument. They argue that physical difference is not a stumbling block for women to take part equally with men in all spheres. Women are full of capacity as like men. But if both men and women are equal, why the scholars use the word 'gender'? Therefore, study about 'sense of gender' is also most important for us. To make sense of gender, we should observe our lives closely, seriously and critically why are people supposed to be exclusively feminine or masculine? A serious effort is necessary to examine the ways in which women have been rendered subordinate to men. We should ask ourselves whether there is anything 'normal' about our world being arranged this way, and if there are other ways of arranging it. I personally never accept any argument which advocates for a normal situation in our world. People are always stratified their sex differences that lead to discrimination and prejudice. Women are being exploited by men in different spheres. So, 'sense of gender' had to emerge in the mind of feminist writers as well as women activists throughout the world. In this similar context, S. Wharton also mentions that the study of gender is sociology grew out of the second waves of the women's movement. She writes "one expression of this movement in colleges and universities was its criticism of academic disciplines, like sociology, for ignoring women. Women were rarely the subjects of research, and activities heavily dominated by women (e.g. housework) received little attention." They introduced the concept of gender into the work of sociologists. According to Sharmila Rege, a noted feminist writer and sociologist, "Across the world, the gender politics of second-wave feminism has been intertwined with the introduction of the concept of gender into the professional work of sociologist" (Rege: 2003). On the other hand, most significant factor behind the rise of the feminist movement was rooted in women's demand for their right and asking protection from any kind of exploitation. In this regard, a huge number of feminist scholars developed their direction towards the social construction of gender in the last thirty years. They sought to establish sex as biologically determined and gender as socially constructed. But debate is not finished over the distinction between sex and gender. The constructionists still are not satisfied with the causes of the sex-gender distinction. Moreover, differences arise over whether one considers these structures in the singular or the plural. The issue of race was central in propelling these debates on gender as multiple structures of power. In this context, several arguments were developed to go beyond class and race as more additives to gender. Of late, gender theorization has converted the focus from material to discursive structures and sociologists have started to analyze the different facets of social construction of gender. While the term 'Gender' gradually starts to enter the sociological discourse, the legacy of the 'add women and stir' approach lingered until very recently. If we look seriously, it is commonly depicted that gender scholars had given more attention to women and any other topics related to femininity rather than to men and topics related to masculinity. They have written more about differences between men and women than variations among women and among men. In this context, Wharton argues that "Perhaps more fundamental was the persistent, often implicit assumption that sociology as a discipline could accommodate new knowledge about gender without having to rethink some of own key assumptions about the social world." The rigidity of definitions and oversimplification of ideas in the context of gender leads to certain stereotypes regarding men and women. While both men and women got attached to various stereotypes, both positive and negative; women on the other hand most often got associated with a number of negative stereotypes. Lindsey writes, "The assignment of negative stereotypes can result in sexism, the belief that the status of female is inferior to the status of male." (Lindsey: 2011). Lindsey also refers to a very important issue in the field of gender studies which is patriarchy. She writes, "Sexism is perpetuated by systems of patriarchy, male dominated social structures leading to the oppression of women." (Lindsey: 2011). Patriarchy, until very recently, has been considered as something inescapable and inevitable; challenging which is one of the primary concerns of sociologists working in the field of gender.

The study of Gender in sociology started in the research on sex-roles. Gender was conceived as an achieved status with a set of gender roles. It was generally influence of functionalism and role theory which are most common discourse in sociology. Generally, feminist sociologists conceptualize gender as a system of relationships that cut across age, race, class and institutional boundaries. They even reject the concept of patriarchy and make an outline of gender order as a site of relations of domination and subordination. It is also noticed that some of the feminist sociologists have tried to re-conceptualize gender by using ethno-methodological approach.

They have put forth diverse positions about privileging the category of gender over women. "The shift from women to gender has been viewed by same as a replacement of the study of sexual inequality with the study of the differences between the sexes. (Evans: 1990). In this way, the sociology of women has gradually given way to changes that has been depicted in a growing literature on men and masculinity. Although men have long been of interest to sociologists, thin recent literature focuses on men as gendered rather than generic beings. This development, in turn, has been accompanied by the relational understanding that what women are or can be, requires attention to what men are or can be.

With regard to recent conceptual development of sociology of gender, a good number of sociologists have discussed it in detail.

With the reference of Connell, Mimmel and Messner, Wharton also rightly takes part in this discourse. She mentions that "The acknowledgement of multiple rather than singular expression of gender has been accompanied by a recognition that some forms of masculinity or femininity are more socially valued than others." In this view, relations between particular kinds of masculinity are understood as relations of domination and subordination. This statement makes the conceptual development of this subject abundantly clear.

Historical explanation of gender is also the most significant to make the real sense of gender. Social scientists discussed masculinity and femininity in diverse ways. Among them, Fredric Engel, Karl Marx, Juliet Mitchell, Gerda Lerner, Sigmund Freud, Jacques Lacan, Karen Horney, Alfred Adler, Carl Jung, etc. are some of the most eminent personalities, who contributed to the gender discourse. The explanations of these social scientists and socio-psychologists also played a significant role for initiating the study the gender issue from different viewpoints in social sciences. Unlike other explanations, these are not expository in nature nor any particular opinion have been given by them regarding existing truth, whether this truth is expressed by religion, Science or Politics, or proclaimed as normative and pragmatic. These explanations are only associated with question of why, how and when did men and women come to be recognized as necessarily different being.

Note

1. Karuna (1990): *The Dialectics of Tradition and Modernity and Women's Education in India*, Vol. 39.

2
Interpretation of Gender

Though we earlier raised the question on the notion of gender, no attempt has been made, however, to interpret Gender so far. Actually, it is a strange word within feminism. Of late, different scholars from different academic persuasions have given its definition in their own ways. But indeed, it is defined in somewhat contradictory roads. Gender is still used as a contrast term to 'sex'. Though 'sex' and 'gender' are interconnected, both convey two different meanings. Even though some form of gender differentiations between men and women have existed and continues to exist in every human society, these differences were, until recently ignored by the sociologists. The reason for this ignorance is that such gender differences are so embedded in the social structure; it is very difficult to see and question their naturalness and inevitability of existence. This ignorance was ended by an explosion of studies, texts and theories which aimed at placing such gender differences in various situations covering a wider social, economic and political terrain. Such an overwhelming interest in the issue brought forward many questions that were hidden until then. In this context, the question arises in my mind, how put into a certain category of male or female constitute the experience of one's life and is such a rigid classification sufficient? Further, it is also very intriguing just to think what social processes might be involved in the formulation and sustenance of such categories. In light of this, I strongly agree with Kath Woodward that gender has been taken for granted in many aspects of social and political life and it is only relatively recently that gender and gender relations have been subjects of scholarly investigations. Thus Woodward has rightfully raised the questions—What is meant by the term Gender and how is it used? What sort of evidence is there that supports the claim that gender is a key determinant of inequalities and of social experience? finally, why does Gender matter?

An attempt to answer such questions has led to the understanding of gender in a number of different ways by different scholars. David Grover and Cora Kaplan writes that "'Gender' is now one of the busiest and most restless terms in the English language, a word that crops up everywhere, yet whose uses seem to be forever changing, always on the move, producing new and often surprising inflections of meaning. We talk about gender roles, worry about gender gap, question whether our ideas are not gender-biased or gender-specific, and we might look for edition information on these and related topics in the rapidly expanding gender studies section of our local bookstore. This rich linguistic profusion is confusing enough, but all too frequently it is made worse by the discovery that many of these neologisms appear to be pointing in sharply opposed direction" (Grover and Kaplan: 2013). This statement by Grover and Kaplan not only points towards the importance and versatility of the concept of gender, but also the inherent contradictions within it. However, the concept of gender is not weakened by the presence of such contradiction, but leads the way for more in depth and varied way of looking at the phenomena of gender discrimination and gender inequality in our society.

M. Bahati Kuumba says that, "Gender is not as straightforward a concept as many believe" (Kuumba: 2003). She mentions the reason for that is first, it is distinct from sex, the physical and physiological feature that differentiates females and males. As opposed to being a biological designation, gender is a social construction—the differentiations and institutionalization of the expected characteristics, norms and behaviours associated with being female or male in any specific social contexts. The category of gender overlaps with various other categories like race, ethnicity, class and sexuality. Defining the complex nature of gender and understanding it as a social category has been an issue of fierce debate and ideological struggle between essentialists and social constructionists. The essentialists believe that the distinctions that exist between men and women are inevitable and natural. They also believe that such distinctions between sexes exist as females and males are biologically determined 'natural' opposites. Thus, the essentialists present femininity and masculinity as mutually exclusive binary opposites. The social constructionists, on the other hand, represent a process of transformation which moves through three distinct phases—from an emphasis on sex differences to preoccupation with sex roles to the centrality of gender (Hess and Ferree: 1987). Thus, the constructionist understanding of gender goes beyond a simple identification of differences between women and men to an analysis of gender as a historically developed social system that operates interactively on social, political, cultural and economic levels.

Judith Lorber understands gender as an institution that acts as a key organizing principle in human social life. It not just represents a structured set of relations, statuses, and norms of behaviour, but also incorporates process, stratification and structure. If we are to see gender as a process, it is necessary to pay attention on the dynamic ways that gendered patterns and relationships are continually constructed and reconstructed through human interaction. The dynamism of gender suggests that we are 'doing gender' that is creating, recreating and reinforcing norms and behaviours connected with gender. As a system of social stratification, gender includes social inequality and hierarchy associated with men and women. Difference and inequality in terms of resources, distribution of power and opportunity marks the ingredients that constitute the gender categories. On the other hand, structural aspect of gender refers to the way in which it organizes social life and divides labour into separate spheres associated with women and men, i.e. the private and public sphere respectively.

The understanding of gender can be initiated with two simple questions: what it is? and what it is not? These two very simple questions bring us to a very important and initial debates in the study of gender in sociology; the sex-gender debate. Gender is cultural while sex is biological. As biological fact, sex is determined much before the birth of the child. But gender is socio-cultural and environmental. It is determined and defined and redefined throughout the evolution of the individual's life. In light of this, we require to understand that sex determines 'maleness' and 'femaleness' based purely on physical differences. So, sex has the structural quality of being universal. Gender determines 'masculinity' and 'femininity' on cultural differences and it is rooted in ideology. From that point of view, it cannot have a universal application. Social scientists have revealed that gender has existed and understood differently in various historical periods and a complete understanding of the term is possible only with the help of an historical contextualization of the same. In a similar way, cultural backgrounds and the position of masculine and feminine exists and changes constantly within the hierarchies of class, caste, ethnicity and nationality. So, it is evident that the degree and the definition of 'masculinity' and 'femininity' shift from time to time, place to place and group to group. Thus, the sex-gender debate highlighted clear distinctions between the two concepts involved. We can summarize these differences in a very concise way:

(i) Sex is a biological phenomenon, but gender is a social phenomenon.
(ii) Sex is the gift of nature which is ascribed. But, gender is a socio-cultural concept. It is achieved and learnt.
(iii) Sex is of permanent nature. The physical attributes of men and women are universal. But gender is changeable. Gender attributes changes from place to place and family to family.
(iv) Sex can be changed, but gender cannot be changed. The term gender refers to the socially constructed and malleable component of human sexuality. Whereas, sex refers to the biological and immutable component of human sexuality.

After going through this initial debate on sex-gender differences, it can be said that gender describes the ideas and the practices that constitute femininity and masculinity. Gender has long been viewed as a legitimate source for the allocation of rights, powers, privileges and responsibilities. In this context, we can identify three important aspects of gender:

(i) Gender trends are not value neutral. The roles, rights and obligations assigned to each sex are not just different, but also unequal with male roles and rights being valued more highly than female roles and rights.
(ii) Gender is not immutable or static. Being socially constructed, gender roles, rights and expectations can change over time and across geographical space.
(iii) Gender involves differences in power, both 'power to' and 'power over'. The concept of power to encompass legal and informal right, access to resources and pursuit of knowledge and personal goals.

Hence, gender should be understood as the structure of social relations that centres on the reproductive arena and the set of practices that bring reproductive distinctions into social process (Connell: 2002). In this context, we can underline three important characteristics of gender which will definitely help in getting a clearer notion of gender in sociological discourse. These are:

(i) Gender equals a fixed state in terms of being a process.
(ii) Gender is not a simple aspect of people. It occurs in every level of social hierarchy.
(iii) Gender talks about its significance in systemising unequal relations.

Gender is socially constructed as opposed to that which is biologically given. From this point of view, 'gender' refers to personality traits and behaviour in distinction from the body. Therefore, it is very clear that there is a clear distinction between 'sex' and' 'gender'. "On the other hand, 'gender' has increasingly become used to refer to any social construction having to do with the male/female distinction, including those construction that separate 'female' bodies from 'male' bodies." (Nicholson: 1995). Here, it is clear that society shapes even the ways in which body appears. But if the body is itself manifested through social explanations, then sex is not something that is separate from gender. In this context, Joan Scott has mentioned in his work, "Gender and Politics of History" that gender is the social organization of sexual difference. But this does not mean that gender reflects or implements fixed and natural physical differences between women and men, rather gender is the knowledge that establishes meanings for bodily differences (Scott: 1988). Therefore, it can be said that whether the distinction between men and women are socially or biologically governed is less important that the way the society is commonly organized around these distinctions. From this perspective 'gender' is considered as a set of social practices which impact on the life of both men and women in our society.

On the other hand, another section of social scientists wished to separate social elements (gender) and physical attributes (sex) distinctly, but indeed, it cannot be separated. Gender includes aspects of sex and meanings of gender are generally based on real observations about the physical bodies or minds of both men and women. Therefore, we cannot consider 'gender' as a replacement for 'sex', but it can be considered as a means to undermine the encompassing pretensions of sex. During the late 1960s and early 1970s, a good number of feminists accepted the premise that "there existed real biological phenomena differentiating women and men used in all societies in similar ways to generate a male/female distinction" (Nicholson: 1995). Thus, 'gender' was accepted as a concept to supplement 'sex', not to replace it. Moreover, 'gender' was not only considered as not replacing 'sex' but 'sex' seemed essential to elaborate the meaning of 'gender'. In this regard Gayle Rubin defined it as "the set of arrangements upon which a society transforms biological sexuality into products of human activity, and in which these transformed sexual needs are satisfied."

Anthony Giddens, a noted modern Sociologist has also strived to separate both gender and sex. He has mentioned that while sex refers to physical differences of the body, gender concerns the psychological, social and cultural differences between males and females. Drawing a very clear distinction between sex and gender from sociological viewpoint, it can be considered that gender is socially constructed concept.

Defining gender sociologically, it may be the easiest way to get the inner meaning through examples based on people's everyday experiences. We have already interpreted differentiation between 'sex' and gender as stated by various social scientists. Primarily 'sex' is referred to anatomical distinctions between men and women made at birth. On the other hand, gender refers to interpretations that have been socially constructed to pierce the arguably 'neutral' facts of gender in one evaluative direction or another. Simone de Beauvoir mentions in his "The Second Sex" that 'facts of biology' cannot explain the universe of distinctions that came, over the course of history and convention, to block women's access to equal participation in all human endeavours (1974). Therefore, from this discussion, it can be said, gender refers to cultural and social interpretation that turn sexual difference into more than biological distinction from sociological approach. Many social scientists use the word 'gender' to show the differences based on anatomical characteristics concerned with sexual differences. The term 'gender' is preferred because it encompasses the social and cultural aspects of difference. Gender is used to focus the social construction of meanings about femininity and masculinity and the importance of social divisions between men and women. This focus on gender as implicated with sexual division makes an understanding of the social and political aspects of sex rather than observing sex and gender as distinct categories possible.

To conclude in the words of Kath Woodward, "The concept of 'gender' now informs a wide range of disciplines and has implications and applications for policy making. Gender is a way of explaining as well as describing social relations" (Woodward: 2012).

Note

1. Rayna R. Reiter, (ed.): "The Traffic in Women" in *Toward on Anthropology of Women*, Monthly Review Press, New York.

3
Concept of Patriarchy

What is the meaning of Patriarchy? It is a question for all in sociological discourse. This particular word means the rule of the father from literary viewpoint. In simple word it means patriarch. As V. Geetha writes, "the term patriarchy means 'the absolute rule of the father or the eldest male member over his family.' This meaning of the term has been extended to describe the nature of this rule. Patriarchy is thus the rule of the father not only over all women of the family, but also over younger and socially or economically subordinated males" (Geetha: 2009). It gives an insight into why women must fight so hard to defeat the power of men. Originally, this word was used to narrate a particular type of "male dominated family". This type of family involved women, junior men, slaves, children and domestic servants who were under the rule of this dominant male. But these days it is being used commonly to refer to male domination, to the power relationships by which men dominate women, and to characterize a system whereby women are kept subordinate in a number of ways. For instance, it is called '*Pitrisatta*' in Hindi, '*Pitratontro*' in Bangla and '*Pidarshahi*' in Urdu. Kamla Bhasin opines that the subordination that experience at a daily level, regardless of the class we might belong to, take various forms — discrimination, disregard, insult, control, exploitation, oppressions, and violence — within the family, at the place of work, in society. The details may be different, but the themes are the same.

Different scholars define this term from their own perspectives. A good number of feminists use the term 'Patriarchy' as a shorthand for male authority and male dominated society. In this regard it describes both power relationships and brings out the interconnections between different areas of life, which are still invisible to many 'male-stream' theorists. Patriarchy is viewed as the bases of women's oppression and the phenomena cannot be understood without others. However, this basic understanding is only the starting point for other feminist scholars who have developed the analysis of patriarchy is a wide range of ways. In this context, different claims are also raised. A few of them strive to identify its linchpin in sexuality, reproduction or the family. Again, on the other hand another group is to focus on employment or the patriarchal nature of state power. Yet one more group has also wished to concentrate on the ways in which patriarchy is maintained through culture or language. It is also noticed that generally feminists use 'Patriarchy' like a concept. As like other concepts; it is also a kind of tools to understand our realities. According to Juliet Mitchell, a most eminent feminist psychologist, 'patriarchy' is to refer to kinship systems in which men exchange women. It is also the symbolic power which is exercised by only fathers within this system. Gerda Lerner (1986) expresses that patriarchy means the manifestation and institutionalization of male dominance over women and children in the family and the extension of male dominance over women in society in general. According to Lerner, men always hold power in all the important institutions of society and that woman are deprived of access to such power. It does not imply that women are either completely powerless or completely deprived of rights, resources and influence. Gerda Lerner mentions that "Patriarchy is a historic creation formed by men and women in a process that took 2500 years till its completion. In its earliest form patriarchy appeared as the archaic state. The basic unit of its organization was the patriarchal family. Which both expressed and constantly generated its rules and values?" Kate Millett, a radical feminist referred to 'patriarchy' as a central concept in her work 'Sexual Polities'. Perhaps one could say that the concept of patriarchy is to radical feminist theory what the concept of capitalism is to 'Marxist theory' (Millett: 1970). According to Kate Millett; patriarchal societies were one wherein, if examined closely, men held positions of power in virtually all decision-making spheres. In this regard Lynn S. Chancer and Beverly Xaviers Watkins mention: "At the time Millett wrote Sexual Politics in 1970, most countries certainly including the United States were patriarchal by this definition."

Sylvia Walby defines patriarchy as a system of social structures and practices, in which men dominate, oppress and exploit. From her definition of patriarchy, as mentioned in her important book

'Theorising Patriarchy', it is very important and significant to understand patriarchy as a system because this helps us to ignore the concept of biological determinism. It also inspires us to reject the concept that every individual man is always in a dominant position and every woman is in a subordinate one. This system is concerned with the particular ideology that men are superior to women, that women are and should be controlled by men and that women are part of men's property. In this regard, certain examples might be depicted from some South Asian languages. These are *Swami, Pati,* and *Shauhar, Malik* which mean 'lord' or 'owner'. Generally, dictionary definition of patriarchy indicates the meaning as the domination of elder males over juniors, males as well as female, in the family, tribe or nation, allied with the considering of descent in the male line. In this meaning, the term came into its own in the second half of the nineteenth century at the confluence of classical legal studies and the emerging discipline of anthropology and, within that later discipline, from the domain of 'social organization', that is, family and kinship, where it was paired with an antonym, 'matriarchy.'

However, the term patriarchy is used in a different sense today. Earlier it was just a descriptive term that explained how specific societies constructed male authority and power. But now patriarchy is also used as an analytical category. V. Geetha says that "the transformation of patriarchy from a descriptive to an analytical category happened in a specific global historical context—the 1970s– that gave birth to a rousing feminist political and intellectual culture in diverse global contexts" (Geetha: 2009). In Indian context the 1970s saw widespread participation of women in the Naxalite movement, the coming of the idea of planned economic development that marked the beginning of NGOs with a significant number of women workers, participation of women intellectuals. In the resistance against the unpopular and authoritarian regime during the period of national emergency, active participation of women in anti-price rise movements in which the poor and unprivileged women joined together for more viable and independent economic option which resulted in the birth of SEWA (Self-employed Women's Association) and such similar participation in many other fronts (Geetha: 2009). This period made sure that women were visible and so were their problems and issues. Such development along with steadily strengthening women studies, which successfully detached women from the 'family' and addressed her as a social entity on her own right; led to a through enquiry of the patriarchal structure which in time revealed the ways in which women in India are subordinated and exploited under this system. V. Geetha writes that "since then, 'patriarchy' has been critically deployed, chiefly to unpack the key constituents of authority and power in any social system, which automatically privileges men over women" (Geetha: 2009).

In nineteenth century, most of the anthropologists dealt with this notion very seriously. According to them, the notion of patriarchy belonged, along with its inverse, 'matriarchy', within competing schemes of universal stages in the evolution of the human civilization and human family which was moderated by cultural diffusion. Again in twentieth century, the paradigm was converted in anthropological discourses. Both matriarchy and patriarchy were reckoned within new models of social organization. In the mid of 1960s, the dictionary of social sciences provided an interesting comment on patriarchy. That is, "The term patriarchy, patriarchate and patriarchal have now nearly disappeared from the vocabulary of the social scientist. They formerly referred most commonly to the governing of a family by an elderly male, although there were other slightly different usages."[1]

It is noticed that anthropology had been preoccupied with debates on the diffusion of forms of the human family since 1860s. A good number of social thinkers had sought to criticize the anthropological interpretation of patriarchy in human civilization. They even consider anthropological interpretation within the so-called structural functional school of British social anthropology. In this context, Patricia Uberoi wants to focus on the dominant mode of kinship studies that have provided a distinctive interpretation of the institutions of matriarchy and patriarchy. Patriarchy is not the same everywhere. A very good example of this heterogeneity of the nature of patriarchy comes from the differences in the societies of north and south and north-eastern regions of the country. Indian society is undoubtedly largely patriarchal in nature. In both north and south India, patriarchal system gives absolute power to the male head of the family. Women in these societies hardly posses any right in the decision making process of the family and even in their own life. However, even though the societies of north-east India are undoubtedly patriarchal, these societies provide its women much higher and dignified status in comparison to the societies in the north and south India. It is argued that, as most of the societies in north-east India are of tribal origin, the status of women is naturally high in these societies. However, in Assam, the society which is not entirely tribal also depicts such trends of moderate or flexible form of patriarchy. The society in Assam, even though patriarchal, is marked by higher status for women, women with right to participate in the decision making process of the family and their own lives. The absence of dowry system in the society of Assam suggests that women in Assam occupy a far better position in the society in comparison to their north and south Indian counterparts. Thus, it can be easily comprehended that patriarchy is not a rigid structure, but is a heterogeneous in nature.

However, even though the nature of patriarchy is different in different classes in the same society, or in different societies and in different periods in history, the broad principles remain the same, which is men's control. But the nature of this control may differ. Here we may specially mention some of the examples of patriarchy in our lives are as below:

(i) Discrimination against girls in distribution of property.
(ii) Preference to a male child by parents to continue family lineage.
(iii) Burden of household work on women and young girls.
(iv) Male control over women's body, labour, property, sexuality etc.
(v) Lack of educational opportunities and other exposure for girls.
(vi) Women were tortured and killed in the name of witch hunting.
(vii) Domestic violence against women.

In Assam, many scholars have completed their research works on different problems of women. These studies are enough to express the examples of patriarchy in this state. J.P. Saikia, in his work "Problems of Education and Rural Women" (2008) has highlighted the problem of education among rural women. The findings of his work focus on the negative attitude of the male-folk towards women education, and lack of aspiration of parents for women education. In the light of this finding, it can be said that discrimination against girls still exists in Assam. R. Saikia (2008) also opines in her work that several taboos discriminating against tribal women have existed in certain tribal groups implying impurity and low status. Kamala Bhasin (1986) mentions that "the feelings and experience of subordination destroys self-respect, self-esteem and self-confidence and sets limits on the aspirations of women. Norms and practices which define women as inferior to men and impose control on women, are present everywhere, in families, social relations, religions, laws, schools, textbooks, media, factories and offices".

However, patriarchy cannot be seen as a simple mechanism that oppresses and exploits women. The nature of patriarchy is very complex indeed. The study of patriarchy so far, has not only pointed to its negative aspects, but also has enumerated its productive nature too. V. Geetha argues that "a patriarchal system provide comforting self-definitions and norms, which, however restrictive and limited, also amply reward those who learn to accept their defined roles as mothers and wives. Wifehood and motherhood are glorified and granted not only social sanction, but also eulogized in literature, art and religion. So, that women do actively want to essay their social role" (Geetha: 2009). Patriarchy is not just subordination of women. Men are also subordinated under this process. Thus, not all men are powerful in patriarchal system. V. Geetha points out that, "in the Indian context *dalit* and 'lower caste' men, men who are oppressed and exploited by the powerful of their sex and denied access to resources as well as their own masculine identity" (Geetha: 2009). Thus, in this way such men are also the victims of patriarchy just as much as are women.

Gendering Caste from a Feminist Perspective

Uma Ckakravarti, a distinguished feminist historian, who has a long association with the women's movement and the democratic rights movements argues that to understand the historical evolution of specific forms of stratification in the subcontinent we need to give male dominance and upper caste dominance not only a historicity, but also a common lineage because both of them are very closely linked. While doing that diversity and heterogeneity of caste and gender according to region must be kept in mind. The relation between geographical region, ecological zones and the forms of stratification is now widely recognized. Intensity of caste system is also affected by this relationship. An evolved caste-based patriarchy is different from tribal patriarchies. Furthermore, various forms of tribal patriarchies have coexisted in close proximity with Brahmanical patriarchies and have been influenced and reshaped by dominant forms of patriarchies in India. The relationship between caste and gender is complex and has not been satisfactorily explored yet. Hence, a more prudent way will be to begin by examining the historical evolution of caste and class and the engendering these processes of evolution. Chakravarti argues that such an approach can bridge the gap between two moments in history. First, from a pre-Manu social formation ranging from the fifth to third centuries B.C. to the structures outlined by Manu in the first or second centuries A.D. Secondly, from that structure to contemporary social reality. The author criticises the structural understanding of caste, provided by Dumont and others as static and unable to take into account the heterogeneity of caste which defines social reality. In the real social process, it is the relations of production and reproduction that defines social groups and not the other way around. Hence, representations from the Brahmanical prescriptive texts must be confronted with lived social reality.

The idea that men hunted and women gathered and this created a hierarchy between the sexes is now contested. Gathered food accounted for almost 60 per cent of the food supply in the prehistoric hunting-gathering societies and women took part in both hunting and gathering as recent archaeological evidences shows. There was no rigid sexual division of labour and women's important role in economy attached more importance to her reproductive roles as the future of the community dependent upon this mysterious power that women possessed. There was no need for sexual control of women by men in such societies. Lack of written evidences from Harappan civilization makes us unable to say anything conclusive about the gender relations in Harappan culture. However, the presence of a complex economy and social stratification and even a strong state makes it difficult to imagine that women's sexuality was not already under some form of control.

Celebration of Rig Vedic period as a golden age for women by the nineteenth century Hindu nationalist, from educated upper middle class, always male and upper caste was because they needed to hide the evidently 'low' status of women at their time. Rig Vedic society was mainly pastoral, largely egalitarian and non-surplus producing. But an analysis of the hymns suggests a strongly patriarchal nature of the society which is fairly evident in the valorization of male war heroes. As economy was simple women were not excluded from production and were involved in cattle rearing which were the source of wealth for the family and community. Women's sexuality was under the control of community. The practice of '*Niyoga*' proves the high value attached to women's sexuality and reproductive labour. Gender stratification existed along two axes—class as well as within the clan to which a woman belonged. Stratification based on lineages suggests the presence of control over women's sexuality within lineages. Chariot driving warrior aristocracy considered senior lineage and marriage could occur within these lineages. In that case control of women's sexuality becomes indispensible. Evidences from Rig Vedic hymns suggested female sexuality within family was considered as something which is dangerous and needed to be controlled carefully. Kumkum Roy's analysis of Rig Vedic rituals suggests that there were two parallel patriarchal forces existed. One was the king who controlled all the productive and reproductive resources of the realm and the other was the male head of the household who controlled female sexuality at the level of family.

By sixth century B.C. Gangetic Valley was witnessing a transition at many levels and Buddhist and Jaina texts are useful in studying in more detail the resultant processes of caste, class and gender stratification. In such texts references can be found regarding dialogues between Buddha and various Brahmanas who claimed highest status in society and right to draw services from the lower '*varnas*'. In such dialogues Buddha contests such claims and it becomes evident that along with contesting these claims of superiority by the Brahmanas, alternate notion on system of stratification is also suggested. In Buddhist texts, the control over land is regarded as making for high status but never referred to by the Brahmanical terms of '*varna*' or '*jati*' suggesting a certain openness of entry to such statuses. Strikingly, the classification into high and low is merely twofold in Buddhist texts, unlike the more elaborate Brahmanical system. There is a rejection of the permanency of categories of owners of means of production and also the permanence of servility. King was not seen as someone who upholds '*varna*' or '*jati*', but as someone who acts vigorously to punish adultery and theft. Family and private property recognized as social institutions instead of a birth-based social order regarded as divine and immutable. Buddhist texts regarded social stratification as dynamic and capable of reformulation. However, in spite of a rejection of inherent status by birth, endogamy in marriage has been mentioned in Buddhist texts too. The author argues that the system of stratification reflected in the Buddhist texts is closer to the actual relations of production at that time. However, the alternative system of stratification that these texts presents probably did not succeed and an alternative to the Brahmana's ideological structure did not emerge. In the Buddhist texts, there is no established link among endogamy, occupational specialization and birth based hierarchy with attendant privileges and disabilities. It was the linking up of these separate elements through the *varnasamkara* theory a handy tool providing an ideological justification for the proliferation of castes within a more complex production system, relying heavily on endogamy and the '*jati*' level to perpetuate the whole structure—that led to the broad '*varna-varga*' congruence that we still have with us.

Manusmriti attempts to establish the *Varna* framework. Maintaining the caste order of statuses, occupation and services is of prime concern. Thus, it seems that *Manusmriti* is trying to legitimize the *Varna* order which is not firmly established yet. Manu tries to make caste order obligatory under the execution and protection of king. He stated that for the survival of the caste system the lower '*varnas*' (*Vaishyas* and *Sudras*) must fulfil their 'obligations' and the king must ensure that they do.

The functioning of performing these obligations by different castes had to be institutionalized and a structure of ritual power, knowledge, political power, occupational division, land control and command over labour had to be established. For this, a structured marriage system became the prerequisite of Brahmanical social order. Hence, marriage has received considerable attention in *Manusmriti*. Manu mentions eight forms of marriage. But they can be divided in two broad categories—Indissoluble sacramental marriage for upper castes and less rigid forms of marriages and remarriages for the lower castes. Manu prescribed endogamy for the higher castes for maintaining purity. However, violations of endogamy existed and to rationalize them came the theory of *Varnasamkara*. It enabled a transition from *Varna* to '*jati*' and an elaboration of caste system where reproduction, production, occupational specialization and distinctive ritual and cultural practices according to caste came to be linked together. Under *Varnasamkara* more castes are born of '*pratiloma*' than the permitted '*anuloma*' unions and the Brahmanas as the purest class are responsible for maximum number of new class through their violations. *Varnasamkara* ensured a steady expansion of the low castes by creating new ones and incorporating them into the

Hindu social structure on the one hand and through making breach of endogamy condemnable for the higher castes it ensured the purity and non-dilution of those higher castes keeping the power with them. *Varnasamkara* was the mean by which caste system could be proliferated and the control over women's sexuality could be differentially organized according to the location of the specific caste in the caste hierarchy. With the help of land grants, the Brahmanas started to spread to different parts of the country and they brought along a new mode of production. New tribes and social groups with distinctive social and economic system, which were most often self-containing, were absorbed into the caste hierarchy and their labour were appropriated by the higher castes. Through the proliferation of the lower castes new labour power were incorporated. But the social ethos of these people were left intact even though they came into the hierarchical caste structure, which ensured the reproduction of labour and a peaceful integration of these new castes into the larger caste hierarchy. In this way, it was not a process of assimilation, but a process of aggregation. Proliferation of the caste system at the lower levels ensured the survival of the new social and economic order which was controlled by the Brahmanas and the kings or the higher castes. Under this process of socio-economic formation caste based patriarchal codes were linked to the production relations of a primarily agrarian society with state backing both the caste system and patriarchal practices of a given region.

As we discuss the concept of Patriarchy which is concerned with male-domination over female in a particular social system; a very significant question may be raised that which areas of females live can be considered to be under patriarchal control. In this context, Kamala Bhasin points out some of the areas as mentioned below:

Women's Productive or Labour Power

In everyday life men control women's productivity both within the household and outside. Women have to provide all kinds of free service to their husband, children and other members of the family throughout their lives. Women's labour is expropriated by their husband and others who live there. Housewives are the producing class, while husbands are the expropriating class; their back-breaking endless and repetitive labour is not considered work at all and housewives are seen to be dependent on their husbands. On the other hand, Men control women's labour outside the home in different spheres. Whether women will do work for earning, it will depend on willingness of men. Husbands compel their wives to sell their labour or they may prevent them from doing work. Even men may decide what women earn; they may selectively allow women to do work intermittently. It is also true that women are forced by men to sell their labour at very meagre wages. Women are kept aside from high paid jobs in organizations.

Women's Production

Men control productive power of women. In many societies women cannot decide how many children they wish, when to have them. Women do not have the freedom to take decision whether they can use contraception, or terminate a pregnancy etc. It is also very unfortunate and miserable plight for women in many societies that sex life of them are being determined by men. Even in context of reproduction some male dominated institutions like the state or church also lay down rules regarding reproductive capacity of women. In modern days, the patriarchal state strives to control women's reproduction through its planning programmes. The state decides the optimum size of the country population. In some countries, women have been urged to have several children. It is only to ensure a sizeable domestic market for the industrial products. Again in some other countries, like Europe, women are inspired to have more children through giving various incentives. As birth rates are very low in these countries, women are provided fully paid job for rearing and bearing of their children. They are allowed for long maternity leave. Some countries even provide for 'male maternity leave'. But in Assam women are being encouraged for family planning to make a sizeable population. Very interestingly Assam government offers five thousand rupees to the women who reproduce only two Childs by giving three years interval. From this situation, we can get the idea about pliable plight of womenfolk in human society. On the other hand, in course of time patriarchy not only compels women to be mothers it also determines the conditions of their motherhood. This is the most useful example of women's oppression. It restricts women empowerment in proper way.

Control over Women's Sexuality

Earlier we have already mentioned that in some countries sexual life of women is determined by men. Women are compelled to offer sexual services to their men according to their desires. The expression women's sexuality outside marriage is fully restricted to because of moral and legal regime. But people are not more interested to turn their eye towards male promiscuity. At the same time men may force the wives, daughters or other women in their control into prostitution, i.e. trading their sexuality. Rape and the threat of rape is another way in which women's sexuality is dominated through an invocation of 'shame' and 'honour'. On the other hand, dress pattern, external behaviour and mobility of women are seriously and carefully monitored to control their sexuality.

Women's Mobility

Proper mobility is highly expected for women empowerment. But in order to control women's sexuality, production and reproduction, men need to control women's mobility. Various customs, traditions and sanctions of human society are making stumbling block for the mobility of womenfolk. Women are still under social compulsion. They cannot move freely as like men in true sense. The imposition of *pardah,* restrictions on leaving the domestic space, a strict separation of private and public, limits on interaction between the sexes, and so on, all control women's mobility and freedom in ways that are unique to them that is, they are gender-specific, because men are not subjected to the same constraints.

Property and other Economic Resources

Candidly speaking through there are the legal provisions about women's right to property, but unfortunately in patriarchal society. Women are not aware of these legal means and they are being exploited for centuries together and considered as the property of their male guardians. Most of the properties and other productive resources are controlled by men. Generally, ownership of property and other productive resources are passed from one man to another, usually from father to son. Legal right to inherit such property is meaningless in patriarchal society. In this way, emotional pressures, customary practices, plain violence, social sanctions, prevent women to achieve real control over their own lives. In other cases, personal laws curtail their rights, rather than encourage them. In all spheres, it is seriously noticed that women are disadvantaged. They are exploited in human society by male through various means. In India, though the planned interventions launched through Five Years Plan and other socio-economic schemes for the welfare of women, but women are still lacking behind of so-called our all-round development. In practice literacy rate of women is still low and their participation in economic activities is not at all satisfactory. They do not have any freedom to decide on their economic activities in true sense. This is amply illustrated by UN Statistics, "Women do more than 60 per cent of the hours of work done in the world, but they get 10 per cent of the world's income and own one per cent of the world property."

We will find patriarchal institutions throughout the world in some form or the other. Among them, family, religion, law, media, political systems etc. are most significant which are all patriarchal in nature. Men control all these institutions. Men benefit not only in terms of greater privilege and control, but materially and economically as well. Patriarchy has a material basis. In this context, Sylvia Walby made a very significant statement. She says women are the producing class and men are the expropriating class. Eminent feminist scholar Heidi Hartmann makes a very close link between patriarchy and capitalism. She expresses, "The material base upon which patriarchy rests lies most fundamentally in men's control over women's labour power. Men maintain this control by excluding women from access to some essential productive resources (in capitalists societies, for example, job that pay livings wages) and by restricting women's sexuality. Monogamous heterosexual marriage is relatively recent and efficient form that seems to allow men to control both these areas. Controlling women's access to resources and their sexuality, in turn, allows men to control women's labour power, both for the purpose of the serving men in many personal and sexual ways and for the purpose of rearing children. The services women render men, and which exonerate men from having to perform many unpleasant tasks, occur outside as well as inside the family setting. The material base of patriarchy then does not rest solely on child bearing in the family but on all the social structures that enable men to control women's labour.[2]

In this regard, it should be noticed that though men generally hold power in these institutions, however, women are not totally powerless without having rights under patriarchy. It can be considered as inequality between men and women. Women do not get equal opportunities as like men. "In fact, unequal system cannot be continued without the participation of the oppressed, some of whom derive some benefits from it. This is patriarchy as well." Nowadays women are being empowered by some legal and non-legal means. Even they have themselves empowered in certain particular areas. They have achieved the power by becoming rulers like Indira Gandhi, Sekh Hassina. They even raise their position in art, culture and literature, but indeed, it is not enough example to say that this change the reality of male-dominated society. Women are merely accommodated in it in a variety of ways. A good number of efforts have been made by women to equalize their position in human society; but they are still under pressure. In capitalists society workers play a very significant role to give a parallel stage for all, they even participate in management to some extent, but does not mean that they are in control. Here we can mention a very important statement which was expressed by most famous social writer Gerda Lerner. She rightly makes an interesting felling point:

> "Men and Women live on a stage, on which they act out their assigned roles equal in importance. The play cannot go on without both kinds of performers. Neither of them "Contributes" more or less to the whole; neither is marginal or dispensable. But the stage set is conceived, pointed, defined by men. Men have written the play, have directed the show, interpreted the meanings of action. They have assigned themselves the most interesting, most heroic parts, giving women the supporting roles" (Lerner).

In this context, how women are valued by men, it is only significant. Women are not absolutely excluded from power and status in patriarchy. Another interesting matter is that women also support the men to perform their activities. Women are also part of the system. They have to internalize its values and not free from patriarchal ideology. They derive some benefits from it. "An equally complex set of relationship keeps their cooperation or complicity as some feminists call it—active." (Kamla Bhasin: 1993). Keeping this view in mind, Gerda Lerner remarks:

> "This cooperation is secured by a variety of means: gender indoctrination; educational deprivation, the denial to women of knowledge of their history; the dividing of women, one

from the other, by defining 'respectability' and 'deviance' according to women's sexual activities; by restrains and outright coercion; by discrimination in access to economic resources and political power; and by awarding class privileges to conforming women... a form of patriarchy best described as paternalistic dominance."

Notes

1. Gould, J. and W.L. Kolb (eds.) 1964. *A Dictionary of the Social Science*, London: Tailstocks, p. 416.
2. Heidi Hartmann, "The Unhappy Marriage of Marxism and Feminism: Towards a More Progressive Union", in *Capital and Class* 8. Summer.

4
Gender Discrimination

Though, in the twenty first century we are talking about male and female equality, it is very unfortunate that we are still not in a position from where we can deny the existence of gender discrimination on multiple levels in our societies with strong conviction. Generally, gender discrimination denotes differential treatment based on sex. Gender points towards the characteristics and temperaments that make one male or female. The values attached to a particular gender are always specific to the culture which that particular person is a part of. Traditionally, value of Indian culture was fully defined and determined by male. Women have always been playing a subordinate role. Therefore, the gender discrimination that exists in most societies has attracted global attention. Women are regarded as the weaker section. They are regarded as weaker compared to men in all spheres of human society. The status of women is still lower in the patriarchal society. If we observe the role of a woman in traditional society, it gives us a very pliable picture. Recently, a historical Bill has been passed in both Parliaments which reserves 30 per cent seats for women in State Assembly and Parliaments. But still it is a question of debate that whether this Bill will be useful to remove the gender discrimination or not. Indian society is still under the pressure of traditional and sanctions which consider women as lower than men. The genesis of gender discrimination lies in the inception of gender distinction. Gender distinction is composed of primarily three aspects which are Power, Production and Cathexis (emotional attachment). The main aim of power in contemporary gender order is the overall subordination of women and domination of men. Gender division of labour are also familiar in the form of allocation of economic tasks which is defined by male supremacy. On the other hand, sexual desire is so often seen as natural, but ironically this so normal sexual desire becomes the backdrop for the discrimination of women folk by men. Yet, when we consider desire in Freudian sense where it is defined in terms of emotional energy being attached to an object, its gendered character becomes explicit.

The status of women, the weaker gender becomes evident in the writings of many, both old and new. It is even said that a woman (in relation to her husband) is like a mother while cooking and serving food, secretary while he is working, servant at his feet, courtesan in his bed and earth — like in forbearance. It proves that discrimination based on sex was in traditional societies. Though during the early Vedic period women enjoyed high status and shared equal rights and responsibilities with men. But it seems with the gradual development of the concept of private property women stated to loose their independent position as well as their rights. They continued to fall lower in the scale till the Code of Manu summed up their position. The father protects a woman in her childhood, husband during her youth and her sons in old age, a woman is never fit for independence. Again the medieval period of Indian history brought further deterioration in their position. With the advent of British rule, a new social era emerged. They brought a revolution in the society by highlighting the problem and status of women in India. But in every respect, women are still seemed to be lagging behind. Therefore, they are pushed in to different categories which are 'backward', but they do not constitute a 'class' by themselves. They are discriminated by men on the basis of their physical fitness. So, sexists believe that people can be understood based on only the characteristics of the group to which they belong, i.e. their sexual group as males or females. In this way, it is observed that most of Indian society, irrespective of caste, religion; are characterized by male dominance. There are several restrictions for women. In modern societies, there are norms which are very binding norms and sanction to control women and to disallow them several property rights and other social privileges. Illustrating this further, Prof. Yogesh Atal mentions that even today, widow remarriage is unwelcomed. The system of *Sati*—a widow being burnt alive on the funeral pyre of her husband—is still alive despite its banning years ago. Girls are still being married at childhood; they are growing up confined to their homes and denied access to education. Therefore, gender discrimination is existing in many spheres of life. Though the Constitutional and legal provisions are imposed in our country to give women proper safeguard from discrimination, but still it is in dark. A girl is considered, in the most patriarchal societies, as a social and economic burden. They suffer right from her birth, even from the mother's womb if the pregnancy is detected during gestation period. (It is now strictly prohibited by government) In patriarchal societies, male are allowed for some ritual duties which are strictly prohibited for women. Only male are responsible to perform all those with utmost social rigidity. As example of those duties are reciting of *Geeta*, giving *mukhagni*, placing *Brundavati* or *Tulsi* and collecting a piece of bone from the pyre and immerging it in the holy River 'Ganga'. As per the Hindu faiths and ethics in India, doing those duties by women is '*paap*' (unholy). On the other hand, etymologically the term '*putra*' means son. But in Hindu culture '*putra*' derives from two different words, i.e. '*put*' and '*tra*'. The word "*put*" refers to '*Narka*' and '*Tra*' refers to '*mukti*' which means rescue. So, a '*putra*' or son is considered as a progeny that can rescue his parent from '*Narka*' or from the birth as human beings and entails them to go to *Swarga*. Thus, from this interpretation, it can be understood that ritually the son is more and more important than a daughter. Although, it is not by any means my intention to say that these ideas and practices are in existence without flexibility. In Assam, incidences of daughters giving *mukhagni* to their fathers point towards such flexibility within the rigidity. Things are changing with time, but it is undeniable that such changes have so far been unable to provide a basis to deny the strong existence of discriminations against women in Indian society.

Indian society is marked by innumerable forms of discrimination based on gender. One most significant aspect of gender discrimination is dowry death that happens due to pernicious behaviour of affinal relatives including their husbands on whom married women can rely. In Hindu society dowry is given on the marriage of daughters on demand from the grooms' family. In this culture, the girls are considered as an ultimate economic burden on their parents. So, generally caste Hindu parents wish to get only male child for making free from the dowry problem. Therefore, many so-called educated and elite people detect the sex of the pregnancy illegally at very early foetal stage. Even if detected as a female one, they terminate the pregnancy. Considering this problem, Medical Termination of Pregnancy (MTP) Act, 1971 was imposed by Government of India to sake abortion of unwanted children. But it is very unfortunate that still this type of abortion is going on without knowledge of concerned legal authorities. It is very sad that we can still remark without the fear of being completely wrong that even among the so-called educated and well established families, it is seen that birth of a son is a far more compelling reason for celebration whereas, the birth of a daughter fails to instigate such urges of joy and celebration and often brings sadness and hopelessness to the family. From this pliable situation, we may depict a picture of sex discrimination in Indian society.

There is gender discrimination in the field of education also. In India, the literacy role of women is much lower as compared to their male counterparts. Women are facing a lot of problems to achieve formal education. Still spending money on the education of female children is considered as wasteful and meaningless expenditure. R.P. Mohanty and D.N. Biswal reported through a very fruitful empirical research that "Traditionally, the female population have been suffering from lower literacy rate than the male population since very long past. Even today the female children are still deprived of their rights on education at household level, especially by their parents. This fact is corroborated below with special reference to two different situations on availing of some sponsored educational opportunities (hypothetical in nature) for their male and female children". Apart from this discrimination against women is in the professions, work place, politics etc. In global context, a good number of works have been conducted by scholars on sex discrimination from different perspectives.

Similar discriminations on the basis of gender are also visible in the field of politics. Men had over the years dominated politics, the art or science of government or the management of the political parties almost in every country. It is only a few decades since women have begun taking interest in politics. Political participation is a very important marker of determining gender equality. This realization has inspired the Constitution of India to provide equal political right to women through the Universal Adult Franchise and also prohibits discriminations on the ground of sex and as we find in the articles 16(1) and (2) provides for equality of any public offices. The process of democratic decentralization through the 73rd and 74th Constitutional Amendments in India have become a revolution in the way of sharing and distributing political powers in the grassroots level (Das: 2009). Despite of such efforts it is still very difficult on part of the women to participate in any political activities. The reason probably is a historical reality that women have hardly taken an interest, let alone active part, in politics. Among those, who are trying to change this reality are being held back by the deep rooted gender discriminations present in our society and because of that it is seen that women representatives in the field of politics are acting as dummies controlled by the male members of their families.

In the mid of twentieth century, female attorneys were openly discriminated in America. In 1999, *American Bar Association Journal* and *National Bar Association Magazine* conducted a survey which revealed that 75 per cent of the black lawyers believed that law firms engage in tokenism rather than in genuine diversity and equality in advancing blacks to partnerships. In this survey it was noticed that 57 per cent of black lawyers believed that minority female lawyers are treated less fairly than white female lawyers. Women teaching in law schools face also some problem throughout world. For example, only 15 per cent female is working as teacher in Harvard Law School when this survey was conducted in 1999. In the different professions, female professions like lawyers, accountants, doctors, teachers, etc. are too victimized by sex discriminatory conduct. Vijay Kumar Gupta cited some peculiar examples of gender discrimination in his work. He talked about Joann Trezza who worked in the legal department of Hartford. When she was in line for promotion to an assistant manager attorney position, the authorities of Hartford rejected her as because she was a working mother. After Second World War some of the companies in USA started to discharge the female employees. For example, The Edwin L. Wiegand Company in Pennsylvania took initiative a policy of discharging female employees upon marriage and of refusing to hire women who were married. Here, we may cite one more example of sex gender discrimination in USA. In 1989, the Association of the Bar of the City of New York formed a Committee to study the issues confronting the city's women lawyers. The committee nominated Cynthia Fuchs Epstein, a senior professor of sociology at City University to explore these issues. He reported that "Women faced prejudices emanating from stereotypical assumptions that often led to the selective assignment of women in connection with certain of the firm's matters. Women lawyers also confronted a 'double-bind'. If they did not exhibit behaviour based on male models, they were branded as not tough enough or insufficiently aggressive, but if they were perceived as tough and aggressive, they were regarded as impaired women who acted like men. This 'damned if you do, damned if you do not' attitude acted as a significant deterrent to the acceptance of women for partnership."[1]

In India, work participation of women is not satisfactory. Still a good number of women employees remain as low as 7 per cent in Central Government, 18 per cent in State Government and about 26 per cent in local bodies (cf. G 01:2000:101). In this regard, report of International Woman's Day 2004 focused a very grim picture of women in the world of work. It clarifies that women still fail to manage their job in good numbers. They are facing higher unemployment rate and get achieve very low wages. It depicts gender discrimination which is evident from the differences prevalent in work participation.

Now, let me talk about the health status, medical facilities and gender. We know as a living creature each and every human being including both male and female have to suffer from different diseases. In fact some of the diseases take place because of age and sex. On the other hand, some diseases are not dependent on these. But under any circumstances diseased persons must undergo medical treatment in due time; otherwise the health condition worsens and this would lead the person to death. But candidly speaking, in some patriarchal societies female patients are not given more importance for proper treatment unless they are very serious. In this way, we also find out a cloudy picture of gender discrimination. There may have many more reasons behind this but negligence of female in case of medical treatment is a kind of discrimination against womenfolk. In this context, R.P. Mohanty and D.N. Biswal pointed out some most considerable reasons. According to them "First of all there is high degree of preference for the male for their all-round welfare in the family. The family members preferably want that the scarce resource be utilized for the health care of male members on priority, since, they are the breadwinners or provides food for the whole family. So, once they fall ill means, the economy of the family would get affected and this would also affect the whole family members in many ways" (Mohanty & Biswal: 2008: 91). This reason is evident everywhere in India. If the both husband and wife suffer from the same disease the wife desires to utilize their resources for the treatment of her husband only. Of course, if the resource is not limited, it may not be true. But indeed, due to limitation of resources Indian women are commonly sacrificing in nature. In the writings of Mohanty and Biswal, they very sincerely mentioned one more factor which is responsible for the negligence of men to treat their female kins or spouses medically are that "Men are more mobile outside for their home than their female counterparts. Moreover, since, they earn and move outside frequently they keep money with them and therefore, they touch the medical professionals either in medical or elsewhere and buy medicines as prescribed by such professionals. But on the contrary in patriarchal societies, women have no liberty to move outside of their home without the permission and help of their men." Keeping this view in mind women is considered as weaker sex and therefore, they are also neglected in medical facilities. It is one of the aspects of gender discrimination in our country. As like other state of our country we may cite some very common social customs and traditions of Assam that give a clear picture of gender discrimination.

One day I heard a person telling that his wife had been taking no bath (*Ga-nodhuwa*) for six months. Literally, he meant his wife's pregnancy of that period, in a sense of mocking the lady's new preparation of giving birth to a baby. This attitude rises some questions — what does the person mean by 'taking no bath' or why does he goes to compare the process of pregnancy to that dirtiness because of unbathing. The answer is very simple in the context that saying so indifferently, the person exposes the male's prejudice and antipathy towards the weaker section like women even in this new century. This attitude has now today prompted the popular Medias like Television and radio to spread advertisement as prepared by governmental agency about pregnancy. For example, the husband asks the doctor about his wife's 'taking no bath'. So, it seems that the governmental agencies also patronage the sponsorship of male's dominant power over the women section.

One more example should be cited here in context of sex discrimination as well as female exploitation. Second marriage (which is known as *Tulani Vivah*) on the occasion of a girl's puberty (first menstruation) is a traditional ritual in the Assamese society. The cause behind keeping this ritual was to inform publicly about the girls suitability as a bride for a matter. But that ritual has become such a pomp and gaiety and the guardians like to observe it in a festive mood. Consequently, this festive ritual may cause a negative effect in the mind of that girl at the crucial time of her entrance in adolescence, which is injustice done to women folk. Moreover, in this period of menstruation, a women is treated untouchable (*akhudi*) and even she is debarred from doing any kind of domestic and religious works.

This tradition has deprived the women folk of their due rights and respects. It is a simple matter from the general view, but from sociological point of view, it is very significant in the impact on social relationship. In this context, we can cite a very pathetic example of a girl named "Mamoni" — living in a very remote village of Sivsagar district of Assam. She comments that she was not allowed to enter the village temple for enjoying a "Bhouna" (religious drama performed in Temple) because of her menstruation, which act affected her deeply upset and expressed her common example, but there are lots of such kinds of examples where the women feel deprived of them because of this type socially constructed rituals. But the question rises — why the deprived women and so-called organizations do not come forward to protest this injustice done to the womenfolk in the name of tradition? It is clear evidence enough that Male-dominance is still going on in our society against the weaker section. Therefore, the mindsets of both male and female in our society need to be studied from sociological point of views in the sense that the women society must be aware of their own rights.

For inclusive growth of a society gender discrimination must be done away with. To be able to do so development in the true sense of the term must reach women and for that to happen development must be practiced and analyzed from a gender perspective.

Note

1. V.K. Gupta (2008): *Gender Discrimination and Human Rights*, M.D. Publications Pvt. Ltd., New Delhi, p. 5.

5
Gender and Development

The notion of gender came into existence when the feminist scholars argued that instead of difference the distinction between the sexes must be looked upon in terms of inequality. It was feminist scholars who brought forth the distinction between sex and gender and presented gender as an entity which is culturally constructed. Thus, gender was theorized in academic discourse by feminism. However, this simple distinction between sex and gender was challenged and further debated within the feminist discourse, especially by post-modern feminist scholars like Simone de Beauvoir and Judith Butler. Gender and development are two terms which are in constant usage in the works of academics and policy-makers and has gained a significant level of attention in recent times. Development is a concept which originated in the West primarily under the political-economic framework. At the very beginning development referred to only one type of development, which is economic development. However, over time development has acquired new meanings and purposes. Bringing gender and development together was the result of feminist scholars who characterized gender relations as relations of inequality and subordination (Sarker: 2006). It did not take much time to understand that the presence of such subordination and inequality is bound to affect the process of development and produce different outcomes for men and women. Hence, feminist scholars have always been trying to make women a visible category in the process of development and gender became the tool for this purpose. A Gender approach necessitates that we recognize that the society is discriminated along gender lines and a realization that the development policies must be formulated accordingly for those policies to ensure that that end result of development process can give way for equality between men and women in society. In this sense, gender, when associated with development, remains not just a concept that represents and explains the unequal status of men and women in society, but becomes a tool to bring such inequality to light and then get them recognized and in the process ensuring innovation of practical solutions to such problems through development process.

Accepting this fact, World Bank commented that gender is an issue of development and effectiveness. It is not just a matter of political correctness and kindness to women. Evidences suggest that when women and men are relatively equal, economies tend to grow faster. Development has the way in which we look at men and women and the relations between them. Development must not stick to just economic development and go on to enhance the quality of life of the people in general. Of course, development must cause increase in material welfare through increased productivity. However, it must also ensure increase in social welfare, education and health; leading to an improvement in life situation. Development must also carry with it increased safety, freedom, opportunity and equal distribution. Thus, development is intended to ensure an overall enhancement of the quality of human life which must not tilt towards one specific gender and must be able to become gender neutral. Development is an all-pervasive phenomenon. The economists call it 'development', political scientists call it 'modernization', for sociologists it is 'role differentiation' and for anthropologists it becomes 'cultural change'. It is important to notice that all these phenomena which development encompasses involve both the genders and sexes. Hence, it is more than just commonsense, rather logical that development must account for the needs and aspirations of both male and female members of the society equally.

Empowerment of Women

The concept of empowerment was introduced at the International Women's Conference at Nairobi in 1985. The conference presented empowerment as a redistribution of social power and control of resources in favour of women. According to the conference, empowerment is a way of challenging and overcoming barriers of one's life through which people increase their abilities to construct their own lives and environment. The issue of women empowerment is of crucial importance in today's world. It has been not only a primary end to the process of development, but a very important mean as well. Empowerment is a multidimensional, multifaceted and multilayered concept. It is a process in which women gain greater share of control over resources that is material, human and intellectual resources which includes knowledge, information, ideas and financial resources such as money and access to money. As a matter of fact, empowerment means moving from a position of enforced powerlessness to one of power. It is a process that enables a powerless woman to develop autonomy, self-control and confidence. It also generates a sense of collective influence over offensive social conditions. Women empowerment is a global issue. The term 'empowerment' emanates from the term 'power'. With the help of empowerment, the change in the power balance can be achieved. Weber defines 'power' as the ability to make others do, irrespective of their own wishes and interests implies the rational aspect of power as it is not inherent, but exists in relationships and hence power relationships are concomitant on changes on power possessors. Some of the feminist scholars like Miller, Star Hawk, Bookman, Mergar have emphasised relational power and empowerment of women refers to this broader perspective. As Kate Young says, "The concept of empowerment refers mainly to entrepreneurial self-reliance or empowering individuals and also empowering people through participation in policy making and planning process" (Young: 1993). Thus, empowerment refers to the ability of a person to think and act freely, to make choices and reach their potential as equal members of the society. It is not concerned with power struggle. To 'empower' hence, means: (i) To give power, authority or authority to; (ii) give ability to or enable and permit. Concept of empowerment emphasises not only increasing the power of the individual, but also the quality of life for the individual. Empowerment is a process of awareness and capacity building leading to greater participation to greater decision making power and control and transformation action (Suguna: 2001). Empowerment aims at making women more aware, socially developed, politically active, economically productive and independent individuals who are able to make informed choices and intelligent decisions in matters that affect them and their nation. Various international agencies have taken keen interest in the concept of empowerment and have attempted to formulate ways to achieve this goal rightfully acknowledging the fact that for a qualitative and inclusive growth, empowerment of women cannot be ignored. The United Nations Development Fund for Women (UNDF) has determined the meaning of the term empowerment as:

(i) Acquiring knowledge and understanding of gender relations and ways in which these relations may be changed.
(ii) Developing a sense of self-worth, a belief in one's ability to secure desired changes and the right to control one's life.
(iii) Gaining the ability to generate choices and exercise bargaining power.
(iv) Developing the ability to organise and influence the direction of social change and economic order, nationally and internationally.

In every society, there are powerful and powerless individuals and groups. This power operates in all fields of life as economic, social, political, religious and education etc. The term 'empowerment' is often used to describe the process whereby the powerless is given a greater share of control over resources and decision making. Therefore, the empowerment is naturally about power and changing the balance of power. Power itself can be simply defined as control over resources and control of ideology (Bhowmik: 2006). Present-day notion of power have evolved in hierarchical, male dominated societies and are based on divisive, destructive and oppressive values. The point is not for women to take power and use it in the same exploitative and corrupt way. Rather, women's empowerment processes must evolve a new understanding of power and experiment with ways of democratizing and sharing power building new mechanism for collective responsibility, decision making and accountability. Similarly, once women have gained control over resources, they should not use them in the same short-sighted and ecologically destructive manner as male dominated capitalist societies (Sharma: 2001). The charter of United Nations declares equal dignity and worth of human persons. In 1993, the Vienna Declaration and Programme of Action proclaimed the right of women. But, social democracy is still a mirage. It is known that hardly 5-7 per cent of women are able to enjoy human rights in the country. However, like the rest of the world, Indian government is also taking up various measures to empower women in all spheres of their lives. The Government had declared the year 2001 as the year of women empowerment. The purpose of this declaration was primarily to create and rouse large-scale awareness regarding women's issues and to ensure active participation and involvement by all women and men as well. However, the women themselves must understand the gravity of their present condition and come out with active participation in the process of empowerment. First of all, they must be aware of their rights and exploitation. Secondly, they must change their own perceptions towards their position in the society and must be able to overcome the challenges that a patriarchal and rigid social structure throws at them. Thirdly, they must employ this changed perception into action in order to be empowered in the true sense of the term.

Division of Labour and Sex

The basic concepts such as nature, labour and the sexual division of labour are used without a critique of sociologists' implicit ideological biases, they tend to obscure rather than to clarify the issue. These concepts have been used to explain social inequalities or exploitative relations as natural, inborn, and hence, beyond the scope of social science. Women particularly, must be suspicious when these terms are used to explain their status in society. They share in the creation and maintenance of life is usually defied as a function of their biology or nature. Therefore, women's household and childcare activities are seen as an extension of their physical make-up. Men and women may be innately different but that does not mean that this fact is particularly pertinent. Masculine and feminine behaviours are relevant as far as they reflect social expectations. They enact different roles because society expects them to act in these ways and rewards them if they do, punish them if they do not. In this context, role theory has little to offer by way of a convincing answer when the questions are raised about the necessities of these expectations. It only allows for the possibility that roles and expectations can be transformed provided one knows how this system works. Again, sociologists and other social scientists are also questioning the way in which social expectations are expressed and enforced. A child acquires its earlier knowledge of its destined role in the family. Parents dress their boy and girl children in different ways. There are different codes of behaviour for boys and girls. Even, boys can run, jump, climb trees, but girls are asked to be more careful. Besides that, in India girls in the poor families are less likely to be sent to school. By the time, a child is six or seven years old it has fairly coherent sense of its sexual identity and expectations which are attached to it.

The society allocates the male and female sexes distinctive attributes and role and people consider these attributes and rules not to be easily exchanged and perform all of these without much thought without particularly being self-consciousness about the ordering the world. Because of such expectations, since time immemorial, work has been divided between men and women on the basis of their sexes.

This is now felt and recognized that women are discriminated in terms of division of labour on the basis of sex. Hence, most nations have declared their support today to the legal, social, economic equality for woman. On 11 December, 1980, United Nations Decade for Women formulated at the Copenhagen Conference of July 14-30 urged all member governments to implement it. The response, however, was very disappointing. A bulletin of the world Conference of the United Nations Decade for Women commented dryly "The fact that only 18 made any mention of women in their speeches indicates according to some observers the levels of priority most Governments attach to issues concerning women" (Leacock: 1981).

The gender division of labour is a central feature of gender inequality, both in its economic aspects and in the social construction of gender identities (Huber: 1991, Lorber: 1994). Economic development in the developing world had differential impacts on men and women and it invariably had been negative for women. Heidi Hartmann expresses that "Capitalism, patriarchy and job segregation by sex that the division of labour by sex appears to have been universal throughout human history. It is hierarchical, with men on top and women on the bottom" (Hartmann). A focus on why and how women are displaced from the men dominated occupations when modernization, technological upgradation and economic enhancement are initiated is important to look upon. Subjugation of women in the realm of work is a very much gendered phenomenon. Significantly, Marx also treated both workers and capitalists as men. Women were rendered invisible, they are absent from the analysis of the labour market on the one hand, and their domestic work and its exploitation is taken as given on the other (Delphy: 1984). Feminists rightly recognize that there is a clear distinction between what many regard to be jobs for men and what people regard as jobs for women. The very fact of variation in what were perceived as 'male' and 'female' tasks underlines that there was nothing natural about such distinctions. But gender divisions of labour are deeper than the words themselves. The fact that women's role at home has often been considered inferior one has probably been acting as a stimulus to generate a desire of sharing in the 'superior' role on the part of the women. Sylvia Walby argues that the domestic labour of the housewife comprises the production of labour power of the husband, herself, and children and other dependents. House wife is involved in an unequal exchange of relationship in which she receives maintenance for her labour — which is most unlike exchange relationship under capitalist relations of production (Walby: 1990). Tasks and activities done by women within the household have never been valued and recognized as having economic value. Instead it is perceived just as a duty which a woman is bound to perform just because of the fact that she is a woman. The invisiblization of woman's contribution inside the home led to the visible recognition of work by men outside the home and women becoming the mere dependent side. The direct outcome of the gendered definition of work is that when women do any work outside the home which is perceived to be based on skills that are practised within the home which are rated low, poorly paid and termed as feminine.

In India society has been tradition-directed for several centuries. The wife tacitly accepts a subservient position in the family and her role in the domestic sphere remains complementary. Meeting the expectations and obligations corresponding to her various statuses within the fold of the family largely occupies her routine (Kapur: 1970). In this context, the caste system in India perpetuates the inequality through certain restrictions. Talking about food, it's the women who take care over the hearth of the family and take care that the caste status of the family is maintained. Interestingly, women play a big hand in perpetuating these inequalities since they are related to indispensable details of these aspects. The basis of the family which is the men-women relationship is gendered, wherein the men are representative of his caste position, his wife is his primary and practical assistant. The role of women in the family is so embedded in tradition and concretized by practice that employment of women creates immediate disruption and impacts upon the family by altering traditional division of labour and sex roles within it. The labour force imposes a number of stresses and strains on women as of like wage discrimination against women, discrimination which women face by reason of male attitudes in the labour force and professional groups, problems relating specifically to the care of home, husband and children which involves the wife and her attitude towards her home, husband and children, moral hazards which paid jobs impose upon women from night work and long hours. The primary tasks of women in almost every society are to teach the basic concepts to their children such as language, ethics, hygiene, manners and religion. It becomes one of her socially defined roles while on the other hand the role of the fathers is chiefly economic and primarily supplementary to that of the mother. Employed women with small children face even more of a distress because of her duties towards her child which compels them to have more absence from work because of worry over the dangers to which children are exposed in their absence.

Although there are obvious exceptions, historically women have not typically held positions of power. Masculine traits are synonymous with power and considered superior to feminine traits. Social role theory, gender stereotyping, family/work conflict, lack of mentoring, the backlash effect and the 'old boys network' are all factors which make-up the hypothetical 'glass ceiling' that women face when trying to reach the most senior positions in their careers. The 'glass ceiling' can be described as an "invisible, but impenetrable barrier which prevents women from reaching senior positions within organizations" (Brewis & Linstead: 1999). Further, these characteristics are not currently rewarded in the labour market or by organizations which may result in women's careers suffering. Men and women are very different physiologically. Hence, it is very normal to raise the question that is possible for women to do everything that men does or *vice versa*. A man will be more suitable for cutting down a tree because it involves physical strength, an aspect where men is usually in a more advantageous position than women. But, saying that it must also be kept in mind that not all jobs require physical strength; but women are most often discriminated in terms of work; whether it involves physical labour or not. What is required, then, is men and women to have respect for each other's work and an ability to value the work of others just the way one values one's own work. Only then the shadow of gender bias and discrimination can be done away with in regard of sexual division of labour.

6
Gender and Sociologists

The debate over the content of the discipline is a never ending one in the field of Sociology. Various sociologists have presented their arguments at times for including in and excluding out certain issues from the scope of Sociology. However, it is undebatable that the founding fathers of sociology expressed the wish to claim that Sociology is a discipline that studies society and human behaviour. If we take this fact into consideration, the question arises; can we as sociologists exclude something from the purview of the reach of our discipline which has even a tiny bit of relevance to human beings? Sociologists in new era have given a comprehensive vision towards gender. They have made its new directions. A rich interplay between gender and other issues like class, race, ethnicity and nationality is demonstrated by some eminent sociologists. No sociologist is found to ignore the topic like gender. August Comte (1798-1857); father of sociology was also concerned with gender. The family was also the place in which the 'fundamental principle' of 'natural subordination of women' was demonstrated (1975: 268). This 'natural subordination', Comte maintained, had 'reappeared under all forms of marriage, in all ages' and was confirmed by biological observations (1975:268). August Comte opined that "Sociology will prove that the equality of the sexes, of which so much is said, is incompatible with all social existence" (1975: 269). Harriet Martineau (1802-1876) also studied about women's subjection and slavery. She also wanted to extend her position on women's rights to the rights of slaves. Herbert Spencer (1820-1903) was in favour of equal rights for women. He opined that women should be emancipated from external restrains in their domestic as well as political lives, in 'Social Statistics' (1850) he clearly expressed that "equality knows no difference of sex. In its vocabulary the word 'man' must be understood in a generic and not in a specific sense" (p. 155). His views on gender were part of his broader concern with Kinship. According to Spencer, gender differences were the result of the struggles of primitive peoples to survive. He suggested that women themselves actively promoted the very danger they fear by preferring stronger, more brutal men. Like many others late-nineteenth and early twentieth century scholars, Emile Durkheim (1858-1917) believed that modern society produced pathological gender relations. For him, gender issue is more serious as it affects the harmony and stability of society. As mentioned earlier, Karl Marx (1818-1883) was also strongly concerned with gender issues. In 'The Holy Family' he observed, "The humiliation of the female sex is an essential feature of civilization as well as barbarism. The only difference is that the civilized system raises to a compound, equivocal, ambiguous, hypocritical mode of existence every vice that barbarity practices in the simple form... Nobody is punished more for keeping women a slave that man himself" (Marx 1845, in Rubel and Manale, 1975:54).

Vladimir Ulyanov (1870-1924) also expected the benefits of a classless society to be extended to women. He considered the 'Woman question' to be a matter of oppression. He stated that "these must emphasis strongly that true emancipation of women is not possible except through Communism. You must lay stress on the unbreakable connection between women's human and special position and the private ownership of the means of production." (1921: 695). Rosa Luxemburg (1871-1919) stood against the gender differentiation in human society. She considered herself as a leader of people, not for particular men or women. She refused to play the traditional women's role in the party. She said that women can get their complete freedom only with the triumph of the socialist revolution and the elimination of their economic bondage to the family institution. Max Weber (1864-1920), most notable classic sociologist also talked about gender. His views on gender were basically connected to his interpretation of power. Weber's wife Marianne Weber was a feminist activist and she influenced Weber to involve in feminist circle in Heidelberg. Max Weber viewed women "primarily as human being and only secondarily as member of the opposite sex". George Simmel (1858-1918) has also given his attention to the dynamics of gender relations. His discussion of changing gender relations was coloured by his aversion to the rigid patriarchalism that characterized much of German society at the time.

As like Herbert Spencer, George Simmel also developed a theory about transformations in gender relations as integral to the progress of modernization. Vilfredo Pareto (1848-1923) viewed women as naturally fickle and promiscuous. He used many references to historical and mythological women in his works. He insisted that there would be women willing to sell themselves. He strongly expressed that prostitution for most women is "a case of 'vanity and love of extravagance' or a case of 'Indolence' for there are those, those in higher social circle... who like this profession the way a hunter likes hunting and the fisherman fishing". Consequently, those reformers who 'Organize leagues' against obscenity and the 'White-slave trade' are misguided. Pareto believed it foolish to "worry to much about the seduction of women and so little about the seduction of men" (1916: 3:1319). Beatrice Potter Webb (1858-1943) discussed gender seriously in her works. She argued that non-discrimination in the workplace is essential. According to Webb, the solution to the 'Women question' was not full equality and freedom. She said that men have a special service as producers, but at the same time women also have a special service as servants of the community, creators of something more precious than commodities, creators of the nation's children. The answer to the women question was the 'endowment of motherhood', making the bearing and rearing of children into an 'art through the elaboration of science' (1873-1924: 1:53). She advised "it will be needful for women with strong natures to remain celibate, so that the special force of womanhood, motherly feeling, may be forced into public work" (1873-1924: 1: 214). According to Charles Horton Cooley (1864-1929), Gender differentiation is natural in the first primary group, i.e. family. He opined that girls are more conscious of their looking-glass-self — "they care more obviously for the social image, study it, reflect upon it more, and so have even during the first year an appearance of subtlety, fineness, often of affection, in which boys are comparatively lacking" (1902:202). Cooley did not give any comment towards women as acceptable for feminist in real sense. He said that boy's imaginations are occupied with things rather than people, and they have a stronger, more complex ego than girl. Cooley maintains that in men this is a 'masterful passion', whereas for women it is a need to be appropriated or dominated. Sigmund Freud (1856-1939) also discussed more on gender but it was based on human sexuality only. Therefore, feminist activists as well as scholars never accept his views towards gender. He opined that women have a weaker ego, greater narcissism, and a stronger need to be loved. He justified the subordinate position of women in terms of their being 'less civilized'. Men undertake the 'work of civilization' requiring that they sublimate their instincts, while women "represent the interests of family and sexual life" (1930:73). In the twentieth century, various discussions about gender had taken place in different sociological writings. Talcott Parsons (1902-1979) very clearly expressed his views towards gender in his most notable collaborative work on family and socialization (Parsons, Olds, Zelditch, Bles and Slater). He and his co-authors reported that "the task leader in families around the world is ordinarily the male or father, and the social-emotional leader is the female or mother" (Adams & Sydie: 2002: 356). Talcott Parsons has given his justification that this arrangement is functional for the social and economic system because it provides a free-floating male labour force that follows the needs of the job market. On the other hand, Robert Merton (1910-1972) avoided to give any ideological comment on gender. He paid less attention to it, but he noted how difficult it is for the women's movement to draw on both white and black women, and how difficult it is for black liberation movement to unite both men and women (Merton: 1972:30).

Modern sociologists such as Nicholas Luhmann (1927-1998) and Anthony Giddens (1938-1991) also talked about gender from their own viewpoints. Luhmann did not carry functional differentiation to the point of Parsons' gender differentiation with males as task leaders and females as social-emotional leaders. On the other hand, Anthony Giddens expressed that modern society has dichotomized reason as a male characteristic, and emotion as female. He clearly mentions that "Women's identities were defined so closely in terms of the home and the family that they 'stepped outside' into social settings in which the only available identities were those offered by male stereotypes" (Giddens: 1991:216). After getting his theory of modern society, it is seen that Giddens is not surprised by women's seeking of new freedoms and opportunities. Change is ubiquitous, and gender role are being fried. The critical theorists of the Frankfort School discussed about gender. Max Horkheimer (1895-1973) and Theodor Wisengrund Adorno (1903-1969) emphasized on the problems for male child in capitalist families. They opined that the mother as the representative of nature was a source of security and comfort the male child in the very early stages of bourgeois capitalism. Women were the enigmatic image of irresistibility and powerlessness. Again Jurgen Habermas (1929) has also paid attention a bit to gender in his works. He overtook the gender implications in relations between public and private institutions in capitalist societies. Since 1930, those who have been contributing to sociology as neo-Marxist, they also discussed about gender. Nicos Poulantzas gives several significant statements on gender, especially in "Classes in Contemporary Capitalism" (1974). He argues that women are double victims of their position both as non-productive, or domestic workers and as exploited members of the workforce. Erick Olin Wright (1947) adds gender to his analysis of class. Wright expressed that a section of scholars are seeing gender as reducible to class and another section views it as reciprocal to class. He strived to understand the most efficient relationship amongst race, class and gender in modern society.

Dorothy E. Smith (1926) and Patricia Hill Collins (1948) also discussed about gender. They were feminist sociological thinkers. Smith explored the political economy of class in relation to gender and Collins analyzed gender in relation race. It is very difficult to separate the gender from race in Collins's work. It is also significant for sociological discourse that a generation in late nineteenth and beginning of twentieth century discussed society and gender very seriously. Charlotte Perkins Gilman (1860-1935) talked about the equality of both men and women. Gilman opined that men and women were born equal and it was "cultural conditions that divide them" (1916:185). She listed the evolutionary; cultural pressures that have produced the excessively sexual and material modern woman. According to her perception, gender is a social construction. She also remarked that economic dependence in particular is the critical factor maintaining modern gender in equality. She also expressed that men and women are the same in intelligence and in ability to contribute to society, Post-modernists in the last part of twentieth century participated in the discussion on Gender. Michael Foucault (1926-1984) had written "The History of Sexuality" in three volumes by which he pays attention to this field. The first volume of this work makes attention to the road in which women's bodies were subjected to control and discipline in modern society. Of late, gender has become an essential part of sociological study. Courses on gender studies are being introduced in the curriculum of the Sociology departments in various universities and colleges. The increased popularity and relevance of the subject has attracted many scholars who are currently working actively in the field of Sociology. Such scholars include eminent personalities such as Iravati Karve, Karuna Chanana, Leela Dubey, Tulsi Patel, Sharmila Rege, Nivedita Menon, Vidyut Bhagwat, Meenaxi Thapar, Rajni Palrewala, Shamita Mannan, Uma Chakravarti, Patricia Uberoi, Rita Manchanda, Beatrice Kachuck, V. Geetha, Maitrayee Chaudhury, Samita Sen, Sumita Sarkar, Padma Valaskar, Pat Kaplan, Rajmohini Sathi, Madhu Nagla and many more. In the north-eastern region of the country, Department of Sociology, Dibrugarh University has been spearheading Sociological inquiry in the state of Assam and the North-East region as well and taking up relevant issues and problems in the region. The department is working over issues such as witch hunting, spousal violence, physically challenged women, reproductive health, family planning, women and sexually transmitted diseases, gender inequalities, women and employment, participation of women in politics, women in development activities, women in family resource management, women and media, sexual harassment, women in medical professions, women in armed conflict situations, women entrepreneurship, women in police profession, gender and health etc.

Sociologists have been contributing to the field of gender studies from different viewpoints. We cannot discuss all in details and it is also not our objective in this chapter. As like sociologists a good number of scholars from Anthropology, Psychology, Philosophy, Woman studies have been dealing with this important discourse. Gender Studies is an unavoidable part of Social Sciences. No one can expect any kind of progressive, equilibrium society without having women empowerment.

7
Gender Theories

The Sociology is reflexively engaged with the object of its study. In the wake of rapid and profound social changes in the late twentieth century, it is important to question whether our theoretical frame of references are appropriate for these transformed configurations of culture, economy and society. Further, sociologists need to raise questions whether recent theoretical preoccupations adequately address the social processes in the millennium. Here comes the question, how do we proceed to relate the concepts from these localised concerns to the concerns of the globalized social world? Gender relations have been the site of one of the major transformation of the twenty first century. We now need to explore the ways in which Sociology can reconfigure the relations between gender, identity and nature. It should also be the prerogative of the sociologists to find out in ways that new configurations will neutralise our social differences, while avoiding simplistic polarizations. In the field of gender studies too, such a rethinking and reconfiguration has emerged as the need of the hour. In this chapter, I have attempted to provide a very brief account on the theoretical developments that have occurred in the field of gender and a retrospection of what should and could be.

What is gender theory? It recognizes equal potential while allowing for differences between the genders. "Gender theory is a more comprehensive feminism; one that includes man, woman, and child. Gender theory investigates the social organization of sexual differences, constructed and/or inherent. Bringing to bear the male condition thus leads to the linkage of gender and feminism" (Channa: 2006: 10). Gender is the attributed normative aspect. Commonly, it is focused around the human concept of sex, a biological physical division which extends to a broad social construction, shaping, informing, limiting ways of being, both feminism and masculine.

"The sex category becomes a gendered through use of gender markers. All aspects of human interaction and human being are gendered." (Channa: 2006: 11) Channa mentions that gender theory is the progression of feminism. Feminism started with understanding and acknowledging the position of women. In this way, Gender theory also wants to understand the role, implications, impacts and potential of male/female interaction. Having said that, I would like to begin with a brief discussion on the very important theories in terms of gender studies which include Marxist theory of gender, queer theory, gender pluralist theory, gender pluralism, feminism and eco-feminism.

(i) Marxist Theory of Gender

This theory has different forms and stresses, but it focuses on its fundamental hypothesis is very clear and coherent: gender is not an isolated piece of reality. I have to be looked in relation to the social whole, to what Marxists refer to as totality. According to this theory, idea of masculinity and femininity are neither normative nor do they exist as categorical imperatives. The roles of male and female cannot be considered as functional. They exist as aspects of a social and economic system. In this context, they reflect social dominance. Actually, we must know the concepts used by Marxists to understand reality for making clarity on gender from Marxian perspective. Marxist theories are reflexive: they constantly seek to question their own premises, because Marxism believes that understanding is a dynamic process. In the opinion of Marxists, human beings make their own lives and they do this through two material processes which are always interlinked. These are production and reproduction. Production consists of all those activities done by members of a society for getting their fundamental needs: food, shelter and clothing. On the other hand, reproduction comprises a specific activity which brings children and raises them to confront with the existing society as other members need. Both production and reproduction are decisively associated because to be able to grow food, or build a house, one needs to survive. Marxists believe that every society organizes production in particular ways. The mode of production is always dynamic, not static. It changes in cause of time.

Modes of reproduction are both cultural and physiological. In this way, it is noticed that women produce children who move on to capture their vested roles in the production system. But women always perform a very significant role in the mode of production. They socialize their children for production process in many different ways. One of the most effective ways of socialization happens through culture and religion. They take responsibility of most family rituals and observe religious functions faithfully. Relationships of production are organized in different societies differently. Again, relationship of reproduction always involves individuals. They do not involve social groups, such as the poor and the rich. There are emotional attachment between men and women. Marriage plays an important role to make the relationship between man and woman. It also constitutes the family for which relationships of reproduction vary from culture to culture. They are more stable than relationships of production. Relationships of production and reproduction intersect at various points. For example, in caste based society, "the marriage relationship in a poor *dalit* labourer's household is vulnerable to disruption by the landlord who, at any time, can demand sexual access to the labourer's wife. Feudal land relationships and the caste system together mark the lower caste women's sexuality as 'available'." In this way, Marxists argued that mode of production and reproduction bring change and give way to new forms. This happens when the relationship of production reaches a point of crisis. Therefore, actions of men and women make reality and that reality compels them to act in certain ways. In this way, Marxism explain how women become subordinate to men.

(ii) Queer Theory of Gender

Queer theory is one of the most significant theories of Gender. This theory was popularized by a section of social thinkers those who associated with the study about the intersections between lesbians and gay academic work in the areas of cultural studies and literature. Queer theory was emerged during the late 1980s and 1990s. Queer indicate Homosexuality. A Queer means a homosexual man. Study about Queer has recently experienced a paradigm shift. It is growing healthy in the contributions of modern scholars who have had the profit of training in queer theory. "Much of the most exciting work in this new moment of Queer Studies refuses to see sexuality as a singular mode of inquiry and instead makes it a central category of analysis in the study of racialism, trans-nationalism, and globalization."[1]

Here, some attempts are manifested to define new fields such as Queer post-Colonial Studies, Queer Ethnic Studies and Transgender Studies. Generally, it is noticed that a section of social thinkers always argue that there are still not more jobs in Queer studies and in recent years an emphasis on queer thematic can often take excellent candidates out of the running for traditionally conceived jobs. But sexuality makes its way on to praiseworthy lists of areas of interests. A considerable number of social thinkers have been dealing with the queer studies in a variety of disciplinary venues since 1980s. But in case of queer theory, it has its roots in post-structuralism which was mostly depicted on the very thought provoking work of Mitchell Foucault. One of the hallmarks of queer theory is the destabilization and subversion of existing categories. Mitchell Foucault, Sedgewick, who are considered as main theorist, investigate the real way in which sexual appetite is made *via* dualistic discourse, therefore, that people are bound to feel that heterosexuality and homosexuality are the only options.

It is noticed that queer theory deconstructs gender and sexual identities, initially *via* interpretations of cultural texts. We can mention one most useful example from the writings of Butler. In his work "Gender Trouble : Feminism and the Subversion of Identity", J. Butler explains cross-dressing and drag as queer and as challenging hetero-patriarchal norms because they enlighten the ways in which gender is constructed. From this viewpoint, it can be considered that gender identities are enacted with the objective of destabilizing the normalization of certain types of gender and sexuality. It also shows that how all genders and sexualities are not genuine. Even queer theory also makes lag for fictitious alternatives to the rigid gender binary system. In this context, R. Dunphy (2000) has rightly mentioned that, "It also invites us to investigate the possibilities of a plurality of masculinities and femininities, of a range of ways of living our lives. In so far as this tends towards an implosion of gender as a useful category of analysis, disentangling sex, gender and desire, queer theory also encourages us to focus on the utopia of a gender free world."[2]

Therefore, we can say that queer theory is to explore the possibility of femininities and masculinities. It can investigate gender and sexual diversity. But although the term 'queer' is useful for knowing gender and sexual pluralism in similar ways, there are difficulties with queer theories. First, J. Butler argues in that "it is only possible to subvert the gender binary system from within the process of repetitive signifying (i.e., the performance of gender *via* appearance), which for her does not include surgical alternation" (Bulter: 1990). So, Butler later on, talks about cross-dressing as radical and trans-sexuality as reactionary. In her latter work she means 'Trans-sexuality' as reinforcing hetero-normative construction of Gender. Secondly, she argues that there are difficulties with the way in which "The newly emerging 'Queer Theory' is an attempt to get beyond the gendered and sexual practices of the social world, yet it continually harks back to those categories which it seeks to undo, male, female straight, bisexual".[3] Therefore, it is very clear that although queer theory wants to destabilize gender and sexual binaries, it fails to move beyond them. Thirdly, "While transgender is defined in similar circles as the transgression of gender norms (Bornstein: 1994), it is also an umbrella term covering trans-sexual people and others, some of whom seek to assimilate within the mainstream. The notion of transgression excludes, or is resisted by, trans-sexual people who identify as heterosexual and assume conventional gender roles."[4]

Eminent social scientist Judith Halberstan deployed participation observation as well as textual analysis in his work which is accepted as queer cultural studies by himself. He suggests what queer life loses when it is wholly accommodated within mainstream ideologies of family. He boldly analyzed the explosion of queer in urban subculture. His main objectives are to examine the ways in which queer communities spend their time that are very different from their heterosexual counterparts. By observing the lifestyle management of queer including eccentric economic practices, queerness can be detached from sexual identity. In this regard we can accept one most significant statement given by Mitchell Foucault that "homosexuality threatens people as a way of life" rather than as a way of having sex. Therefore, "at a moment when so many middle-class gays and lesbians are choosing to raise children in conventional family setting, it is important to study queer life modes that offer alternatives of family time and family life."[5]

From this discussion, it is very clear that queer studies are most significant for understanding gender as well as sexual pluralism in our society. Therefore, queer theory is most important for better understanding of gender issues from sociological viewpoint.

(iii) Gender Pluralist Theory

Rigid gender binary is destabilized and provokes a number of questions: Is gender diversity likely to be contained within male/female categories, by expanding these categories? Is it possible to move beyond gender altogether? Is a gender plural system emerging, in which male/female categories are complemented by other identities, and if so how can this be theorized? These questions are discussed by different theoretical approaches, which Surya Monro focuses as mentioned below. Whichever approach is taken, key concepts concern:

(i) *Intersectionality*: as shown above, gender and sexuality operate in complex, contextualized, and changing interaction with other forms of social stratification such as nationality, age, ability, 'race' and ethnicity, and class/socio-economic variables;
(ii) Gender and sexuality as made up of a number of different biological, psychological and social factors;
(iii) Gender and sexuality as the result of a combination of essentialist and constructed process. These processes are ultimately contingent and temporary; and
(iv) The importance of political context and implications, degendering and having plural sexes/genders is strategies that are rejected by many transgender and intersex people.

In this theory, the discussion of the expansion of male and female categories is important. The elasticity of gender binary categories provides gender diversity to be subsumed into 'male' and 'female' at least to an extent. "Expanding the gender binary categories involves theorizing femininities and masculinities as diverse, including people who have bodies or social roles that are different to those traditionally associated with women and men. The expansion of binary categories is conceptually concerned with masculinity studies. Therefore, the understanding of masculinities as plural is most useful and helpful to theorize gender and sexual diversity. There are limitations to the 'expanded gender binaries' model which can be illustrated by looking at the nation of female masculinities."[6]

J. Halberstam in his most praiseworthy article, "An Introduction of Female Masculinity: Masculinity without Men" published in a volume, namely "The Masculinity Studies Readers" explains a range of female masculinities and masculine heterosexual women. This very particular explanation of gender critically erases non-binary trans-sexual identities. It is also problematic for co-optioning of what can be seen as transgress and positive identities that are arguably female, not male. On the other hand, it will be more hard and complex to characterize, if masculinity is unlinked from male bodies. Masculinity in some developed and developing countries inevitably conjures up notions of power and legitimacy. Therefore, the delinking of these characteristics from masculinity would be a worthwhile project. Again, one more problem with the expanded binaries model is that it is not able to include those people who fall more fully outside of the gender binary system. It will defuse the potential for gender pluralism as some alternative identities are subsumed into 'male' and 'female'. But it is also true that a good number of people with diverse sexualities to achieve social rights and acceptance in human society.

(iv) Gender Pluralism

Gender is seen as being more finely grained that is the case with the binary system, and as being formed *via* the interplay of different characteristics associated with gender and sexuality we can get a clear idea about a theoretical strategy which is concerned with conceptualizing gender as plural.

J. Halberstan (2002) mentions that Gender pluralism involves "calls for new and self-conscious affirmations of different gender taxonomies". It concerns with conceptualizing gender as 'groupings' or 'fields'. In some particular cases, it also overlaps femininities, masculinities and gender diverse identities. There are other used pronouns for people who consider them as alternative to male and female pronouns, i.e. 'ze' and 'hir' (Feinberg, 1996). This acceptance of more gender possibilities also means that the categories of 'lesbian', 'gay', 'bisexual' and 'heterosexual' cannot encompass all sexual orientation options. These complementary terms are supposed to become more widespread. Gender pluralism could also mean the extension of categorization beyond the term 'trans'.

Gender and sex as a spectrum was discussed by some of the most prominent scholars. M. Rothblatt in his work "The Apartheid of Sex: A Manifesto for the Freedom of Gender discusses 'gender continuum theory' which is away from bipolar sex/gender categories towards a multiplicity of genders. The concept of a gender and sex continuum may be expanded. In this regard, it can be noticed that one non-trans or bisexual contributor explained gender as places in space rather than a continuum. There are lots of debates on the viability and advisability of a plural gender system. A section of people are talking about 'third gender', but at the same time, another group of people argue that it is not the right time to think about the right of third and other gendered people as we have to fight against some other problems. After all it can be said that "necessitates the exclusion of intersex, androgynous and multiple sexes/genders as socially viable identities".[7]

(v) Feminism

On my part it is very difficult to express precisely what feminism is. The early edition of *Oxford English Dictionary* defines the term feminism as a state of being feminine or womanly as did the 1901 edition of the *Dictionary of Philosophy*. But, by 1906, *The Dictionary of Philosophy* defined feminism as a position favourable to the rights of women (Singh: 2009). On the other hand, the *Webster's Dictionary* defines the term 'feminism' as (a) the principle that women should have political right equal to those of men; and (b) the movement to win such rights for women. Again, Toril Moi has also given a very interesting statement. She says, the word 'feminist' or 'feminism' are political labels indicating support for the aim of the new women's movement which emerged in the late 1960s (Moi: 1986).

After going through the different statements on feminism, I personally realized that unlike many other 'isms' feminism does not derive its theoretical and conceptual base from any single theoretical formulation. Even we cannot find a single person who has defined feminism for all of us for all time to come. Therefore, definitions of feminism have and might change from time to time and situation to situation. The reason is that feminism is based on historically and culturally absolute realities and levels of consciousness, perceptions and actions. Of late, sociologists and other social scientists seriously observed two very significant definitions of feminism which are being accepted by women from India, Bangladesh, Nepal, Pakistan and Sri Lanka. The first definition is that feminism is an awareness of women's oppression and exploitation in society, at the place of work and within the family, and consciousness action to change this situation. The second definition is that feminism is an awareness of patriarchal control, exploitation and oppression at the material and ideological levels of women's labour, fertility and sexuality in the family, at the place of work in society in general, and conscious action by women and men to transform the present situation. From these two definitions, it can be understood that anyone who recognizes the existence of sexism, male domination and patriarchy, and who take some action against it is a feminist. Of course, these definitions give us a very clear understanding that a mere recognition of sexism is not enough, it has to be accompanied by action, by challenge to male domination, but these actions can take any form. Therefore, men can also be feminist, although some never recognize it because they believe that feminism has to be based on personal experience of discriminations. They generally consider male as superior, but not as feminist.

Feminist theory articulates a new kind of knowledge which is constructed by rendering visible the previously invisible components of gender in all discourses produced by the humanities and social sciences. Feminist concepts attempt to analyze and state the material conditions through which gender has been constructed within a specific bodies of literature. The strong wave of 1960s and 70s helped theorise a women's discourse. In 1980s, feminism concentrated on transforming the intellectual field, and in 1990s, started playing a key role in directing academic focus on the concern of 'otherness', 'difference' and 'question of marginality'.

Feminism is a movement that confronts the abuse of power and seeks equality and justice and it aims at changing the way we think about men and women. In modern usage, the term 'feminism' is linked with the women's movement. Feminism has also worked towards improving the social status of women throughout the world. Thus, feminism can be considered as a socio-economic and political movement which rests upon two basic premises: First, women are disadvantaged because of their sex and second, this disadvantage can and should be overthrown. Feminist consciousness questions how gendering reinforced by patriarchy is internalized through the process of socialization that in turn supports and sustains patriarchy. Feminist theory thus tries to locate reality of society through women's experiences. There may be a number of different feminist theories. However, the aims of these different theories have a form of cohesion in their nature and we can mention the basic aims of all the feminist theories as:

(a) Ending patriarchal oppressions.
(b) Evolving women's identities beyond the 'other' of male positions assigned to women by patriarchy and its gendered identity creations born out of biological determinism.
(c) Integrating women's insights into social vision.

As it is comprehensible, it is not possible to do justice to the range of feminist theories and approaches. To define the word 'feminism' in very precise way is also not easy. Even Writer Rebecca West confessed in 1913 that he himself had never been able to find out precisely what feminism is. Again during that time, the word was also not more known to all. It had only appeared in English from the French in 1890. In Germany, feminism is socialistic. Therefore, we have to discuss only its brief outline which is mainly concerned with gender categorization. It is also noticed that some of the writers are commonly using an alternative term instead of feminism, i.e. 'Womenism'. They are not in favour of the word 'feminism'. In 'A Room of One's Own', Virginia Woolf sharply attacks on this word. She rejects the word 'feminism'. Moreover, let us explore some of the major theoretical dispositions to understand concept like gender within a broader theoretical framework.

Liberal Feminism: Liberal feminism advocates equal rights for women which originated in the eighteenth century. It is completely concerned with individual equal rights. Detailed interpretations of feminism are given by authors such as R.R. Tong (1998) in his work "Feminist Thought: A More Comprehensive Introduction." That as the 'mainstream's face of feminism, it involves a focus on achieving equal rights *via* reform, particularly in the public sphere—legal, institutional and political struggles for equality (Beasley: 1999:51-52).

Liberal feminism is based on the idea that people are created equal and should not be denied quality of opportunity because of their gender. Therefore, sometimes it is called as egalitarian feminism. Liberalism is founded on a belief in the importance and independence of the individual and that individuals have some particular innate rights which must be protected both by and from the government, and that freedom is greatest good. Mary Wollstonecraft was the first philosopher who advocates liberal feminism. Mary Wollstonecraft has argued that equality of rights and opportunities should be extended to women in all spheres of life. Liberal feminism is exemplified by the National Organization for women who were formed in 1966. Initially liberal feminism was also highly criticized. Especially in the mid-1970s, it was rejected as bourgeois white women's movement, but later on, scholars and feminists started to change their negative perception towards liberal feminism. As a result, it has brought significant changes in life of women. Liberal feminists make their key efforts to bring social change through the construction of legislation and regulation. They realized that traditional laws and behaviours are main obstacle for women to get equal right with men. According to them, primary block to equality is sexism. Liberal feminists opine that "sexist attitudes about appropriate gender role expectations for men and women continue to lead to discrimination and prejudice against women" (Delaney, Tim: 2005: 205). Liberal feminists advocate that inequality stems from the denial of equal rights. If women are not serious to exercise their rights, they will be hampered badly. According to liberal feminism, individuals are autonomous beings. Women should be treated equally to men. Now a days, liberal feminism is being considered as mainstream feminism. It is fully concerned with equal rights, which include women as well as the liberal values of liberty, equality and justice. In the writings of liberal feminists, they mention that women are discriminated because they are always judged first as women and only second as human beings. It is very miserable perception for womenfolk. They wish to eradicate this type of discrimination through legal means.

Radical Feminism: While liberal feminism had its own history in movements for social reform, radical feminism developed in relation to the radical civil rights movements of the 1960s. It is closely concerned with the women's liberation movements. It maintains that sex/gender system is the fundamental root cause of women's oppression. Radical feminism begins with the insight that gender distinctions, usually unrecognized and unquestioned as they are assumed to be 'natural'; structure every aspects of our lives. "Instead of examining the traditional political institutions in the public sphere for the answer to why women are universally opposed, radical feminists declared the 'personal is political' and examined the way human reproduction is controlled and socialized through such institutions as marriage, compulsory heterosexuality and motherhood. Reforms in the public sphere – surface equality – will not touch the deeper oppression: radical feminists seek to create an entirely new social system" (*Encyclopaedia of Feminism*, 1986). Radical feminism considers patriarchy as a sexual system of power in which the male possesses superior power in different spheres. Men use sexism as the ultimate tool to keep women oppressed. It stresses that male superior power is the basis of social relations. Rosemarie Tong (1989) explains that radical feminists commonly agree with the following:

(a) That women were historically, the first oppressed group.
(b) That women's oppression is the most widespread (it exists in all societies).
(c) That women's oppression is the deepest (it cannot be removed as potentially social classes can be removed from society).
(d) That it causes the most suffering (for example, false consciousness).
(e) That women's oppression provides a conceptual model for understanding all other forms of oppression.

According to radical feminism patriarchy is emerged to control female's sexuality. Catherine Mackinnon (1982) mentions that men always attempt to control the women bodies through the creation of norms of acceptable sexual behaviour. As per his feminist perspective, sexuality is the primary sphere of men's power. Kate Millet has rightly said that the root of women's oppression is buried deep in patriarchal sex/gender system. She argued that sex is political primarily because of male-female relationship is the paradigm of all power relationships. Men control the public as well as private world by making various norms in society. So, radical feminists stand against all existing social structures. They believe that men create everything for their own sake only. For instance, organized religion generally teaches that God is a 'He', and that He is so remote and aloof that he dwells in a place, heaven, that is beyond earth, reminding us that ultimate power over also implies absolute separation from (Tong, 1989). Of course, radical feminism is also not free from criticism. Although radical feminists are achieving their own position in the feminist community, some of them are criticized for their claims about the goodness of women's nature and the evilness of men's nature.

Socialist Feminism: Whereas radical feminism observes the

oppression of women as the result of men's control of female sexuality and the patriarchal institutions that structure gender system and sex, socialist feminism sees women's oppression as stemming from their work in the family and the economy. Socialist feminism strives to remove the both class and gender by combining the insights of radical feminism with Marxist analysis. They believe that women's inferior position in society is the result of class-based capitalism. It is quite similar to Marxian perspective and on the other hand they also think that 'personal is political' as like radical feminism. Indeed, socialist feminism was emerged only for dissatisfaction with classical Marxist perspective on family and women.

They broaden that Marxist perception of the material base of society to include all aspects of what is sometimes called reproduction. Recognizing that the structuring of sexuality, marriage and the family are basic to women's oppression, socialist feminist believe in the importance of challenging the norm and practicing alternatives in their own lives.

They wish to draw components of the radical, Marxist and psychoanalytic insights under one roof. This perspective has given one serious attempt to accept socialist principle to both the home and workplace in order to hike up gender equity. Socialist feminists such as Iris Young, Nancy Fraser and Alison Jaggar argue that gender social position will be changed only through a transformation of the economic system, along with a change in the way household work is evaluated. It shares with Marxist feminism the position that oppression of women is an economic fact, but it is supplemented by demands for ideological transformation in how women are treated in the private sphere.

(vi) Ecofeminism

'Ecofeminism' a term which was coined by Francoise d' Eaubonne in 1970 in Paris. Eaubonne was a famous French feminist born on March, 1920 and expired in 2005. Ecofeminism is a philosophy and movement is a result of the union of feminism and ecological thinking. It believes that the trend of the domination and oppression of women is directly connected to the trend of abuse of the natural environment. In gender discourse, a discussion regarding ecofeminism today is of utmost relevance. It brings together eco-anarchism and bio-regional democracy with strong ideal of feminism. Eco-anarchism is a school of thought within anarchism which puts a particular focus on environmental issues. Bioregionalism is a political, cultural and environmental system or set of views based on naturally defined areas called bio-regions or eco-regions. Ecofeminism state that, a linkage between women and nature exists that arises out of their shared history of oppression by a patriarchal society. This linkage also has its roots in the positive identification of women with nature. Feminist environmentalists study women's and men's differential interests in natural resources and processes caused by their different roles in daily work and responsibility. Ecofeminism is a social and political movement referring to the existence of considerable commonality between environmentalism and feminism with some link between deep ecology and feminism. Ecofeminism is a philosophy and social movement which is concerned about environmental conservation and its improvement. Ecofeminism argues that the oppression and subordination of women in families and society and the degradation of nature has a common basis for their existence. Both form of domination and exploitation are carried out through construction of differences into conceptual binaries and ideological hierarchies which allows a systematic justification of domination by subjects classed into higher ranking categories over those in lower ranking categories. But, there are various contradictory stands within ecofeminism. However, each stand strongly believes that nature can be used as a tool to understand women's oppression. They argue that the mutual devaluation of women and nature leads to a denial of women's activity and the whole sphere of reproduction. Ecofeminism has contributed a lot to activist struggle and theorising. Last three decades have brought the links between domination over nature and women's oppression into light. Plumwood strives to develop the theoretical understandings of environmental degradation along with the continued devaluation of women's reproductive activities. This is achieved by questioning the 'dualistic rationality' of mainstream scientific philosophy. Plumwood has also tried to explore the differences and continuity between feminism and ecofeminism (Datar: 2011). One explicit difference lies in the way feminists view the idea of a feminine connection with nature. This school considers this association as regressive and insulting as it summons images of women as passive, reproductive animals limited to their bodies and an unreflecting experiencing of life. A basic difference between the two schools of thought, as she observes it, is that Ecofeminism accepts the concept of 'equality' uncritically.

The 1960s and 70s was marked by an attempt on the part of the feminists who attempted to fit women into the masculine identity, which was marked by the ability to transcend and control nature. The evidence of this transcendence and control was men's explicit link with mechanization and technology. Plumwood argues that, trying to fit into this image of masculinity is futile and Ecofeminism believes that "women cannot be accommodated into cultural ideas, which has defined itself in opposition to feminine traits (reproduction and caring)" (Datar: 2011). Plumwood also argues that, the 'reversal strategy' of cultural feminists to add positive value to feminine and natural cannot solve the problem of 'equality' because Plumwood believes that the problem lies in the "epistemic concept of dualism embedded in the masculine knowledge system, which constructs 'difference' using a hierarchical logic" (Datar: 2011).

Ecofeminism in the West developed through primarily four different paths. The first path rejected the Marxist assertion that domination is based solely on money and class. The second path that led to Ecofeminism was the exposure to nature based religion. The third path into Ecofeminism came from environmentalism. This path is credited to the publication of Rachel Carson's Silent Spring who fought against pollution and degradation of nature. The fourth path is attributed to women with careers in public policy, science and technology, environmental organizations of public interest and environmental studies programmes in universities. They talk about the need to create a culture which will focus on the interconnectedness of living systems and the interdependence between human beings and nature (Datar: 2011).

Over a period of time there have emerged a number of different trends within the ambit of Ecofeminism. Such trends include Liberal Ecofeminism, Cultural Ecofeminism, Social Ecofeminism and Socialist Ecofeminism. Liberal feminism is rooted in the ideas of liberalism and capitalism as the optimal economic structure for human progress. It also believes that a society to reach it optimum when each individual will achieve his or her maximum individual potential. Thus, they believe that if provided the opportunity, women can also move beyond the social stigma of their biology and join men in creating a culture of coexistence with by conserving it. Cultural Ecofeminism is a response to the view that women and nature have been mutually devalued and exploited in Western culture. They see the connection between women and biological reproduction as a source of women's empowerment and ecological activism. Social Ecofeminism believes that the idea of dominating nature comes from domination of human by humans. They envision a decentralized community which transcend public-private dichotomy, essential to capitalist mode of production. Socialist Ecofeminism assumes that non-human nature is the material basis for all life and it requires food, cloths, shelter and energy to sustain. Hence, they feel the need for humans to establish sustainable relations with nature. But, what is significant is that socialist feminism does not consider nature as a passive object to be dominated, but rather an active subject. It stresses upon social and ecological transformations and socio-historical construction and transformation of nature and human nature. Thus, Ecofeminism, as the newest branch of the feminist discourse provides a fresh standpoint to analyze women's present plight in our society.

As it is mentioned earlier, we are not to discuss about feminist theory in details in this chapter. Apart from these, some other feminist theories are also taking their esteemed places in the discourse of feminism. Post-modern feminism, psychoanalytic feminism and other feminism also develop their own perspectives. Post-modern theory and its assumption that we no longer live under conditions of modernity, but of post-modernity. Kristine Baber and Colleen Murray (2001) explained that a "Post-modern approach stresses the importance of historical context, variations among people and the expectation of change over time. Post-modernism provides a sophisticated and persuasive critique of essentialism rejecting the reductionisms and naïve dualism that results in dichotomous, either or thinking and embracing ambivalence, paradox, and heterogeneity." (pp. 23-24). Kristine Baber and Murray Collen (2001) mentioned in a thought provoking article "A Post-modern Feminist Approach to Teaching Human Sexuality" that "Such an approach encourages a careful consideration of taken for granted information; helps students understand their experiences, even if they are contradictory or incoherent; and is committed to providing information that will be personally and professionally useful to students" (p. 23). They used post-modern feminist approach to teaching human sexuality courses. On the other hand, Psychoanalytic feminists have been found within Freud liberating as well as oppressive streams of thought.

After all, it can be said that a considerable number of feminists contributed to this areas from their own perspectives. Feminist social thinkers contribute to contemporary feminist theory with their deep observation towards gender diversity and sex discrimination in modern complex societies.

Notes

1. Essed & Goldberg (2009): *A Companion to Gender*, Backwell: Kobayashi Publishing, p. 66.
2. Dunphy, R. (2000): *Sexual Politics: An Introduction*, Edinburgh : Edinburg University Press, p. 32.
3. Plummer, K. (1995): *Telling Sexual Stories: Power, Change and Social Worlds*, Routledge, London.
4. Monro, Surya (2005): *Gender Politics*, Pluto Press, London, p. 33.
5. Judith, Halberstam (2005): *Queer Studies*, p. 67.
6. Monro, S. (2005): *op. cit.*, p. 36.
7. M. Surya (2005): *Gender Politics*, p. 39.

8

Gendered Bodies: A New Insight

Gender studies have been acquiring new aspects and meanings every day. Simultaneously, old ideas and accumulated knowledge have also been revisited and are being questioned. Microscopic observation and analysis of seemingly 'normal' phenomena have become a hallmark of gender studies which is accompanied by a trend to redress the existing contents. The human body, today, is not limited to the purview of biology. Sociology and social sciences are taking up the task of studying not only the human body and its organs, but also their movements, acts and the meanings they convey. In this context, the gendered body has also become an integral part of the plethora of subjects the gender studies seek to understand and analyse. Bodies are central to debates about gender. Each individual has a body, each individual is a body and bodies are key markers of gender. The body of every individual is the determinant of their sex, even if the gender may vary from culture to culture. Different societies may perform gender differently, but gender has a close connection with bodily characteristics. What we do with our bodies and how we do that are also gendered. We live in our bodies, but that experience is affected by the images of bodies that we see in the media. However, bodies are not just about biology and anatomy; they are also not just about images and presentations. An individual can always intervene and change how he or she perceives his or her body. Interestingly, bodies are material entities. The body eats, bleeds, feels pleasure and pain, cry and sweat. Human beings do born and die. But, the process of experiencing one's existence through the body does not belong to the material sphere. Embodiment, as we call this process, is a combination of the material and the realm of perception. Many of such experiences are related to reproduction. For instance: menstruation, pregnancy, childbirth, lactation, menopause etc. which are experienced by female. However, the experiences related to the body, both material and perceptive, also have social and cultural meanings and values attached to them. These experiences are the result of social forces outside the body. For example: they are affected by economic systems, the distribution of food, work, education, medicine, sexual customs etc.

The actual material of the body is formed through its interaction with environment. Archaeologists are able to ascertain the gender of the skeleton by analysing the size and shape of the bones, which are different in males and females. Thus, even the material aspects of our body are also gendered. Anne Fausto Sterling argues that, the social world that people inhabit, for example—in terms of nutrition and lifestyle; is embedded in their bones, with women's bones having a significantly different composition from men's (Sterling: 2005). This brings forth new questions regarding differences and the ways in which men might be able to carry other embodied differences that have only recently been identified. Another aspect of material bodies is how they move and what they do. For example, in the field of sport, attributes attached to the body is substantially gendered which has their source in the bodily inequalities between men and women in terms of size, anatomy, muscle power, body mass and stamina. Such attributes have also been linked with psychological characteristics such as aggression. Thus, our material bodies can never be truly separated from the ways in which they are represented, made visible and the meanings that are attached to them which form the experience of embodiment. People are constantly presented with images of what is appropriate for them. These images are most often sexualized, especially when it comes to women. Although, masculinity is catching up and now popular culture displays sexualized images of young men in the same way.

It is seen that feminists from the middle of 1970s have been concerned with how women's bodies are represented and the influence that such images have in shaping gendered bodies. The second wave of feminism transformed protests into campaigns against the concepts like Miss World and Miss Universe. They considered such concepts as explicitly gendered in nature which presented women as sexualized beings. Today, the discipline of Sociology is concerned with the issue of body, and the subsequent meanings and symbols that get attached to it, just as much as were its classical predecessors. Indeed, it seems that the 'body and sexual practices' as socially constituted and changeable with changing assumptions regarding what is 'natural' or 'normal' and what is not. In other words, they have a history and geography (McDowell: 1988). What the sociology of the body focuses upon is that the body and physical experiences are of central importance to individual and social life. Moreover, while the ways in which we see illnesses or the process of ageing may change over time and culture, our perceptions and our experiences pertaining to the body are the result of constant interaction between the culture and the biology.

Foucault and his radical ideas have been important catalysts in generating Sociologists' interest in the human body. He explored the ways people thought and behaved with respect to a variety of activities and behaviour in all of which the human body plays a central role. His phenomenal work 'History of Sexuality' similarly traces of links between physical activities and what could seem more straightforwardly physical than sexual acts. He also studied changes in the way people think and the effect of the underlying structures of power on them. Foucault argues that, we have a simplistic view that people used to be repressed sexually and no longer are. But, human history is far more complicated than that. As we see in the case of homosexual relationship between men and young boys, in classical Greece, this was marked by 'intensity', 'seriousness', 'vitality'. However, by the Roman era, attitudes had changed. But it was not the 'taste for boys' that changed, but this change was marked by a fading of the importance placed within the philosophical and moral debate. Foucault advocates that modern society is characterized by the extension of administrative rationality which devises methods of control which regulates the people.

Debates about the extent to which physical characteristics and behaviours are socially constructed or biologically given have consequences that go well beyond the academic discourse. One of the most significant recent examples of how theories influence public perception and policy is to be found in the area of mental illness. Thus, the question of a 'gendered body' tags along with it a number of other questions that have already been raised in the field of gender studies by sociologists, social scientists and feminists. The important thing which must be noticed that the idea of a 'gendered body' provides a promise of potential to supply a new perspective to look at various previously identified problems and make visible new ones.

9

Female Sex and Protective Measures

Women are called *'stree'* in India which is derived from the verb "*stru*". It means spread. So, the woman is to spread love to the world. Veena Majumdar rightly mentioned that "Man and Women are the two wheels of the cart. If a cart is to run well its wheels must be equal. From the point of view of anatomy, out of 48 chromosomes, there are 47 common chromosomes among men and women (V. Majumdar (1978: 15). In the Vedic period, if we analyze the position of women in the society, it is quite satisfactory. During this period, the position of women could be considered as equal to that of men. As a matter of fact, women enjoyed respect and regard in the society during this era. They enjoyed freedom in selecting their mates. They had got opportunities to educate themselves. The family life provided her the status of "*Ardhangini*". Women had no restrictions in carrying out their social life. Even there was no restriction on women to take up any economic activity. But the status of women in Indian Hindu society underwent enormous changes during the medieval era. The medieval period is called "Dark age" by many scholars as the country had not witnessed any development in most of the areas of life. On the other hand, much change took place in first half of the twentieth century. This period was more crucial as women had gone through the "Dark age". During this period most of the progressive measures were taken by British rules as well as some Indian social reformers. The British regime had played a significant role in bringing about changes in the life of women. The British rule supported various attempts made by social reformers and much legislation was also enacted to abolish certain social evils. After Independence many positive measures were taken for any sex discrimination in India. As mentioned by R.P. Mohanty and D.N. Biswal that after Independence of India, constructive measures were thought to be taken up for the socio-economic prosperity of the nation, the age-old gender issues came into the forefront as great social hindrances against achieving the projected goal. It was decided unless prejudices like unequal social status of men and women that deprive women of their human rights, discriminate and commodify them for the benefit of the stronger sex are legally wiped out; it would not be possible to gain the goal in time. In this regard, necessary legislations have been introduced from time to time depending upon emerging demands. The Constitution of India incorporates many provisions to protect the interests of women. Apart from the Constitutional provisions, many State Governments have also taken different measures to empower women. Therefore, the provisions which have been taken for empowerment and upliftment of women are described in three broad headings as mentioned below:

The Constitutional Provision

The Constitution of India has not provided only legal equality of women with men but it has also inspired the state to adopt positive discrimination in favour of women. The Constitution has guaranteed the fundamental rights for ensuing equality to all before law. A good number of articles of the Constitution of India provide specific provision for upliftment of women. For example, Article 14 guarantees equality of men and women before law and provides equal protection to both of them by the laws. Article 15 restricts the state not to discriminate against any citizen on the grounds of religion, sex, race, caste, place of any them. Even Article 15(i) directs the state to have any special provision in favour of women and children. Article number 16 of the Constitution guarantees equality of opportunity for all citizens irrespective of sex in matters relating to employment in any organization under the state. Again if we look into Article 25, it is seen that this particular Article prohibits traffic in human beings as well as forced labour in respect of women, female children and others. Article 39 directs the state to make policy towards securing for men and women equally the right to an adequate means of livelihood. Article 42 also directs the state to make provision for securing just and human conditions of work and for maternity relief. Article 243 of the Constitution of India is very significant for upliftment of women. Article 243D (3): It is concerned with the reservation of women in Panchayat elections and it specifies that not less than one third of the total number of seats to be filled by direct election in every Panchayat to be reserved for women.

Article 243D (4): According to this article, into less than one third of the total number of offices of chairpersons in the Panchayat at each level to be reserved for women. Article 243T (3): It speaks that not less than one third of the total numbers of seats to be filled by direct election in every municipality to be reserved.

Article 243T (4): It is related with reservation of offices of chairpersons in Municipalities for the Scheduled Castes and Scheduled Tribes and Women in such manner as the legislature of a state may, by law, provides to this effect.

The Legislative Measures

Apart from above Constitutional provisions, the state has also imposed various legislative measures to uphold the Constitutional mandate at the various levels. It provides some special commitments for welfare of women folk in Indian society. "Such legislative measures have certainly intended to ensure equal rights to women and to counter all forms of socio-economic discrimination and violence and atrocities committed against them." (Mohanty and Biswal: 2008: 100). Even some legal support services have been provided for giving proper protection to the working women who are discriminated and harassed at their working places. It is also noticed that women are also being victimized of various crimes in India. Now, crime against women is a very serious matter. In this way, the crimes against women are classified into two categories as mentioned below:

(a) The Crime identified under Indian Penal Code (IPC), which includes cases relating to rape, kidnapping, abduction for different purposes including sexual purpose, Homicide for dowry, dowry deaths or attempts taken to die because of dowry torture, torture, molestation, sexual harassment, eve-teasing, importation of girls up to the age of 21 years.

(b) The Crimes identified under protection of all citizens irrespective of their sexes since crimes are of many nature and these could be committed to any of them. Some of such special laws are mentioned below:

   (i) The Employees State Insurance Act, 1948.

   (ii) The Plantation Labour Act, 1951.

(iii) The Family Courts Act, 1954.
(iv) The Special Marriage Act, 1955.
(v) The Hindu Marriage Act, 1955.
(vi) The Hindu Succession Act, 1956.
(vii) The Hindu Adoption and Maintenance Act, 1956.
(viii) Immoral Traffic (Prevention) Act, 1956.
(ix) The Dowry Prohibition Act, 1961.
(x) The Maternity Benefit Act, 1961.
(xi) The Medical Termination of Pregnancy Act, 1971.
(xii) The Contract Labour (Regulation and Abolition) Act, 1976.
(xiii) The Equal Remuneration Act, 1976.
(xiv) The Child Marriage Restrain Amendment Act, 1979.
(xv) The Criminal Law (Amendment) Act, 1983.
(xvi) The Factories (Amendment) Act, 1986.
(xvii) The Indecent Representation of Women (Prohibition) Act, 1986.
(xviii) The Pre-natal Diagnostic Technique Regulation and
(xix) Prevention of Misuse Act 1994 (cf. GoI, 2000: vi-vii and Behura and Mohanty, 1999:110).

These legislations are concerned with both social and economic sectors.

10
Gender Budgeting

Budget is a very important aspect of overall development and prosperity of any country. A good budget must address to different problems of various sections of people to ensure a seamless growth and development of the country. In the last few decades, it has become abundantly clear that women constitute one of the most deprived, exploited and vulnerable sections of society. Hence, it becomes imperative that special measures be taken to solve their problems. In this context, budget has the ability to act as an important tool in the hands of the state for taking up policies in the form of affirmative action for improvement of gender relations through reducing the existing gender gap in the development process. The process of preparing budgets which incorporates special measures to address the problems and issues of women can be termed as gender budgeting. It can help to reduce economic inequalities not only between men and women, but also between the rich and poor as well. Hence, the budgetary policies need to take into account the gender dynamics which operates in the economy and in the society. Today, the need has been felt throughout the world to highlight and augment participatory approaches, bottom up budget, child budget, green budgeting, local and global implications of pro-poor and pro-woman budgeting and inter-linkages between gender sensitive budgeting and women's empowerment. In order to accomplish these, we must understand the relationship between macro-economic policies and the union budget, state budgets and local self-government institutions in the context of economic reforms and globalization as it influences women's lives in several ways. It is a good economic sense to make a national budget gender sensitive, as this will enable more effective targeting of government expenditure to women specific problems and reduce the negative consequences of previous fiscal policies. The gender budget initiative is a policy framework, methodology and set of tools to assist the governments to integrate a gender perspective into the budget as the main national plan of public expenditure. Gender budgeting also refers to facilitation of required attention to gender analysis considering the macro-economic performance, ministerial budget preparations, parliamentary debate and mainstream media coverage. Budget impacts women's lives in several ways. It can directly promote women's development through allocation of budgetary funds for women's programmes or reduce opportunities for empowerment of women through budgetary cuts. Hence, Gender budgeting is now considered to be a vital tool to successfully address women's problems and fulfil their specific needs. Gender budgeting is gaining increasing acceptance as a tool for engendering macro-economic policy making. The Fourth World Conference of Woman held in Beijing in September 1995 and the Platform for Action that it adopted called for a gender perspective in all macro-economic policies and their budgets. The Outcome Document of the UN General Assembly Special Session on Women held in June 2000, also urged all the nations to mainstream a gender perspective into key macro-economic and social development policies and national development programmes. Importance of adopting gender budgeting was also emphasised by the Sixth Conference of Commonwealth Ministers of women's affairs held in New Delhi in April 2000. In India, till 2004, the process of gender budgeting was just an initiative to analyse and prevent any undesirable gender specific consequences of the previous budget. But 2005 onwards, the conditions changed considerably. Due to consistent efforts by the gender economist and woman groups; for the first time in 2005, the Ministry of Finance gave a mandate to all ministers to establish a gender budgeting cell by January, 2005. At present 54 ministers and departments have formed gender budget cells and have provided annual reports and performance projects highlighting the budgetary allocations for women. The first gender budgeting statement (GBS) in the union budget 2005-06 included 10 demands of grants. In 2006-07, the GBS got expanded to 24 demands of grants under 18 ministries/departments of the Union Government and 5 Union territories. During the financial year 2009-10, the GBS covered 34 demands of grants under 27 ministries/departments and 5 union territories.

The genesis of gender audit of budgets in India lies in various studies, reports and plans which initiated the awareness required for gender specific budgeting in India. Some of such initiatives were the towards equality report, 1974, National perspective plan for woman, 1988 and the Shram-Shakti Report. The Sixth Five Year Plan brought the issue of women and development to the forefront, the Eighth Five Year Plan commented that "the benefits of development from different sectors should not bypass women and special programmes one woman should complement the general development programmes. The later, in turn, should reflect the greater gender sensitivity". The Ninth Five Year Plan introduced the Woman Component plan and commented that "not less than 30 per cent of the funds/benefits are embarked in all women's related sectors".

Gender budget analysis can help to focus on these neglected aspects; it provides women with the vital information regarding the contents can focus on existing government policies. Armed with that, women can confront policy-makers and demand changes in the policies as per their needs and choices. The process is for greater transparency and for deepening of democracy. However, we can still observe serious gender gap in five critical areas which are economic participation, economic opportunity, political empowerment, educational attainment, health and well-being. Historical neglect and institutionalized hegemony is a deep-rooted problem in India which is playing a crucial role in increasing the gap between formal equality and substantive and equality for women in the country. Among the victimized women in India, women belonging to the categories of *dalit*, tribal women, disabled women, Muslim women and HIV positive women are the most marginalized.

Gender budgeting is not a separate budget for women, but it is a part of the government budget to establish its gender differential impacts and to transform and translate gender commitments into budgetary commitments. The main objective of a gender sensitive budget is to improve the analysis of incidence of budgets, to attain more effective targeting of public expenditure and to offset any undesirable gender specific consequences of previous budgetary measures. South Africa was one of the first countries who followed and initiated the formation of the gender sensitive budget in 1995 through participatory process of involving parliamentarians and NGOs. The commonwealth initiative to integrate gender into national budgetary processes was started in 1997 in four countries other than

South Africa which were Fiji, Saint Kitts and Nevis, Barbados (the Caribbean islands) and Sri Lanka. Several other nations have also taken steps to engender their national budget—UK, Mozambique, Namibia, Tanzania and Uganda etc. Gender budget initiatives are currently being attempted in 84 countries following diverse paths in terms of the process and partners involved in undertaking the activity.

11
Gender and Societal Problems

The modern era starts from 1500 A.D. onwards. Many changes have taken place during this period. The social life of women has undergone considerable amount of change. Participation of women in political and economic life has got very significant improvement. The attitude of people to recognize women on par with men has been favourable. Most of these changes have not only improved the status of women, but also the conditions of life. However, these improvements and changes have also made women to face certain problems.

Over the last few decades, there has been a significant increase in the number of working women. All those who work outside home have the problem of managing the demands at the work spot and also to fulfil the expectations at home. It is not only in terms of allocating time, but also in terms of expectations from the members of the family. In nuclear families, the problem is much more serious as she will be alone to shoulder all the responsibilities. At times, this may lead to role conflict and dissatisfaction. On the other hand, the working women will have to adjust themselves at home as well as in work place. This involves multiple roles and varied social positions. There will be many more role demands. At times, these factors may create problems to a woman in adjusting to a particular situation at home or in the work place.

It is common statement that Constitutional measures and legislative protections to women have improved their social status. But in true; the problem has been traditional role of expectations. This may be contrary to her own expectation in terms of aspirations and hopes. She may also assert herself in this direction and claim individuality in family life. Such a situation leads to conflicts within the family.

It is also noticed that many efforts have been made to educate women and to protect their interests through legislation. This has not been duly supported but public opinion favouring equality of status to women. On the other hand, most of the legislations have not been imposed effectively as the general public is apathetic. Another most serious problem is that traditionally has persisted at the community as well as family level. This has confirmed subordinate role to women rather than to allow her claim of equality. This is also true of the literate and educated women of our country.

Above all some of the most significant societal problems also have been concerned with gender. As we have already discussed about gender, it is socially constructed. It is the social organization of sexual difference. Gender is not accepted as a concept to supplement 'sex' not to replace it 'sex' is essential to elaborate the meaning of 'gender' only. Therefore, gender consists of socially constructed concept. It indicates male, female and third sex. From this view; we have to discuss some of the societal problems such as sexual harassment, homosexuality, lesbianism, sexually transmitted diseases etc.

Sexual Harassment

Sexual harassment is a form of sex discrimination that violates Title VII of the Civil Rights Act of 1964. Generally, there are two different form of sexual harassment, i.e. unwanted sexual contact and a hostile work environment. A good number of sociologists, social psychologists, and social thinkers have given different definitions and interpretations of sexual harassment, but it is not an easy task to define sexual harassment. It is a subjective concept and experiences of women are infinitely variable and also open to alternative interpretations. Some women may undergo sexually harassing experience but may not look upon these as harassment. She may be considering the motivation of the harasser. H.C. Ganguli (1988) mentions that some incidents described by the women as harassment may mean something quite different from harassment as understood by social science researchers, or government administrations. In general, two terms have been accepted in India to get the notion of sexual harassment, i.e. 'violation of modesty' and 'eve-teasing'. But these two terms are not enough to define the meaning of sexual harassment. In the shorter *Oxford English Dictionary*; the verb 'tease' is defined as "to worry or irritate by persistent action; to disturb by persistent petty annoyance, out of mere mischief or sport; to bother or plague in a petty way." Therefore, the term "eve-teasing" leaves out most of the severe acts of annoyance and covers only such behaviour as deliberate touching, mild pulling of the *Sari* or whistling or leering.

Sexual harassment is unwelcome attention of a sexual nature. It includes a range of behaviour from mild transgressions and annoyances to serious abuses, which can even involved forced sexual activity (Dziech: 1990 and Poland: 2002). Sexual harassment is considered a form of illegal discrimination in many countries. It is the product of the deep-rooted makes desire to humiliate and put down women who do not fit in with their notions of property. Sexual harassment as defined by the Apex Court is unwelcome sexually determined behaviour as physical contact and advances, a demand or request for sexual favour, sexually coloured remarks, showing unwelcome physical gesture, verbal and non-verbal conduct of sexual nature.

Here unwanted, unreciprocated and unwelcome are the words which differentiate sexual harassment from normal behaviour. When any unwanted, unwelcome or unsolicited sexual conduct is imposed on a person who regards it as offensive or undesirable, it is sexual harassment.

There is a biological basis to sexuality as because of female anatomy is not same with the male anatomy. On the other hand, the experience of organism is also different. There also exist a biological imperative to reproduce; otherwise the human species would become extinct. From this human beings have a wide range of sexual tastes and may follow these even when in a given society, some are regarded as immoral or illegal.

It is also true that sex is a need of human beings; but people can not violate the social regulation in this context. They should maintain the social sanction to fulfil this need in society. Nobody can force others for their own satisfaction. Without the support of his or her partners, if one wishes to get his sex pleasure, then it is considered as abuse or harassment in civilized society. In this fact, the sexual abuse is a widespread phenomenon and much of it happens in the society. Therefore, sexual harassment of women can most easily be defined as the carry out of sexual acts by male. This sexual harassment gives women more pain physically as well mentally. Victimized women loose their faith on the social norms which lead to the disconformities of a society, so the actual morality and ethics are essential to save the womenfolk from sexual harassment.

The term "sexual harassment" was coined in 1974 at Cornell University (Patai : 17-19), however, it was the United States Supreme Court confirmation hearing of Clarence Thomas and Anita Hill's testimony, that brought the issue to national attention in the US (Dziech: 1990). According to Barnes V. Train (1974), the first sexual harassment case was reported in America, but it was not termed as sexual harassment. William V. Saxbe established sexual harassment as a form of sex discrimination in 1976. Sexual harassment can occur in a variety of circumstances. In this context, a good number of social scientists and psychologists discuss from different views. U.S. Equal Employment Opportunity Commission mentioned some of the aspects as mentioned below:

(i) The harasser can be anyone, such as supervisor, a client, a co-worker, a teacher or professor, a student, a friend, or a stranger.
(ii) The victim does not have to be the person directly harassed, but can be anyone who find the behaviour offensive and is affected by it.
(iii) While adverse effects on the victim are common, this does not have to be the case for the behaviour to be unlawful.
(iv) The victim can be male or female; the harasser can be male or female.
(v) The harasser does not have to be of the opposite sex.
(vi) The harasser may be completely unaware that his or her behaviour is offensive or constitutes sexual harassment or may be completely unaware that his or her actions could be unlawful. (Adopted from the U.S. Equal Employment Opportunity Commission).

Sexual harassment is an unwanted and unwelcome behaviour. Therefore, it affects an individual's life chances and lifestyle. Sexual harassment can affect an individual's work or any other activities and can create an intimidating, hostile, or offensive environment. Effect of sexual harassment can vary depending on the individual, and the severity and duration of the harassment. Often, sexual harassment incidents fall into the category of the 'merely annoying'.

Boland (2002), Koss (1987) discuss seriously about effects of sexual harassment. Boland mentions that every year sexual harassment costs hundreds of millions of dollars in lost educational and professional opportunities, mostly for girls and women. Indeed, chronic harassment may also psychological effects on individual. Some of the effects may be cited here as found by social scientists and social psychologists:

(i) Sexual harassment effects on the teaching-learning culture in side and outside the educational institutions. It decreases school performance and increases absenteeism.
(ii) Sexual harassment harms work culture. It makes bar for career and decrease income.
(iii) Individuals are humiliated by this type of unwanted behaviour. Sexual harassment decreases productivity and increases team conflict.
(iv) Sexual harassment occurs as a result of an act or omission by the crisis in morality and ethics of the human beings. It violates moral code of human society. Sexual harassment increases health care cost and sick pay cost because of the health consequences of harassment.

Sexual harassment creates mental disturbances amongst individuals. It even affects life cognition as well as volition. The victims avoid doing deep thinking and stop working hard for the holistic development of society. In short, the person ceases to play the part that she was supposed to play as a part of the society.

Some of the social psychologists have pointed out certain psychological and health effects that can occur in someone who has been sexually harassed. These are:

(i) Depression,
(ii) Stress and Anxiety,
(iii) Sleeplessness and nightmares,
(iv) Loss of motivation,
(v) Headaches, stomach problems, and eating disorders,
(vi) Feeling betrayed, angry and shame.

Apart from these, following common effects on the victims are also seen in our society:

(i) Having to drop courses, change academic plans, or leave school.
(ii) Having one's personal life offered up for public scrutiny the victim becomes the 'accused', and his or her dress, lifestyle, and private life will often come under attack.
(iii) Defamation of character and reputation.
(iv) Loss of trust in environment similar to where the harassment occurred.
(v) Extreme stress upon relationships with significant others sometimes resulting in divorce, extreme stress on peer relationships, or relationships with colleagues.
(vi) Loss of trust in the types of people that occupy similar positions as the harasser or their colleagues.
(vii) Loss of recommendation in all spheres.

So, it is observed that sexual harassment has become ubiquitous. It has become a crisis phenomenon. From this viewpoint, sexual harassment is a very important social problem. Sexual harassment makes crisis in morality and ethics. In this regard a study was conducted in Nazira sub-division of Sivasagar district of Assam in 2001. The objectives of this study were as follows:

(i) To focus the crisis of ethics and morality through sexual harassment.
(ii) To find out the nature of sexual harassment.
(iii) To find out the impact of sexual harassment on the moral and ethics of a society.
(iv) To examine the attitude of women towards sexual harassment.

It is common knowledge to all that in India, crimes against women are increasing. Women are raped, teased and molested. It is duty of every responsible person to prevent sexual harassment by restoring moral and ethical knowledge amongst the people. Awareness among them towards this type of problem should be created. Therefore, study of this crisis is most significant to make an ordered and civilized society at present time.

The respondents in this study were working unmarried women between 25 to 30 years age in different organizations. Total number of the respondents was thirty (30). The study revealed that all respondents are from nuclear family. Out of total respondents,

20 (66.7%) are the follower of Hindu religion. In this study, 18 (60%) respondents became victim of sexual harassment. As many as 10 respondents, i.e. 55.6 per cent became victim of sexual harassment by their colleagues in the offices. Out of 30 respondents, 5 (27.8%) respondents were harassed by passengers in travelling and 3 (16.7%) respondents found sexual abuse from their own cousin brothers. It was also found that all respondents had negative attitude towards sexual harassment. They believe it as a crime. But they never disclose it publicly. Here even 6 (33.4%) respondents, those who became victim by their colleagues in the office, never complained as they fear that such complaints may deprive them of their promotions or may create a hostile work environment. On the other hand, two respondents even confessed that they have already lost their good faith to their relatives also. According to them male easily cross the boundary of human relation and can violate all human norms for their sex-satisfaction. This study showed that nature of sexual harassment focuses in the different forms: (i) Trying to kiss or touching the body, hair and dresses; (ii) Telling sexual jokes or stories, verbal abuse, making sexual comments about a women's body, asking question about sexual life; and (iii) Making sexual gestures with hands or body movements, displaying sexually suggestive posters, pictures, magazines or other objects in the work place.

Candidly speaking no more studies have been conducted on sexual harassment in Assam. But case of sexual harassment is going up throughout the country. It is more in global context also: Approximately 15,000 sexual harassment cases are brought to the US Equal Employment Opportunity Commission (EEOC) each year. The European Women's Lobby reports that almost 40 per cent to 50 per cent of female employees have experienced some form of sexual harassment or unwanted sexual behaviour in the workplace. In United Kingdom (2006), a governmental study revealed that 2 out of 5 sexual harassment victims are male, with 8 per cent of all sexual harassment complaints to the "Equal Opportunities Commission" (Britain's EEOC) coming from men.

Type of Sexual Harassment

In this context Dziech, Billie Wright, Weiner, Linda, L.M. Boland, Leedy Laura, Orit Kamir and Jane Gallop have studied very seriously. They have conducted some of the empirical studies in different countries regarding its nature, types, effects, causes etc. They even categorize the harassers. Boland (2002) in his work "Sexual Harassment: Your Guide to Legal Action" expressed that there is usually more than one type of harassing behaviour present, so a single harasser will often fit more than one category. Now, we have to mention here the different types of sexual harassment as discussed by abovementioned sociologists and social psychologists. The types of harassment can be categorically mentioned as below:

(i) ***Power-player***: It is a kind of harassment where the harasser insists on sexual favours in exchange for benefits they can dispense because of their position in the hierarchy. Getting or keeping a job, favourable grades, recommendations, promotion, credentials, orders and other types of opportunities.

(ii) ***One-of-the-Gang***: This type of harassment occurs when groups of men or women embarrass others with lewd comments, physical evaluation, or other unwanted and unwelcome sexual attention. Harassers may act individually in order to belong or impress the others or groups may gang up on a particular target.

(iii) ***Groper***: In this kind of harassment, harasser wish to insist on kisses or hugs and sometimes involving grabbling the women's breast or buttocks. Even some female harassers ask male about their penis.

(iv) ***Situational Harassment***: In this harassment, harassers start their behaviour when the perpetrator endures a traumatic event, or starts to experience very stressful life situations such as martial problems, psychological problems or divorce. The harassment will usually stop if the situation changes or the pressures are removed.

(v) ***Confidante***: This kind of harasser approaches the subordinate as a friend and wishes to share their own life experiences and difficulties. They even invent stories to win admiration and sympathy for their sexual favour. They invite the subordinate to share their experiences as to make them feel valued and rusted. The relationship turns into a close domain in no time from which the subordinate finds it difficult to separate.

(vi) ***Bully***: In this regard, sexual harassment is used to punish the victim for some transgression, such as rejection of the harasser's interest or making the harasser feel insecure about themselves or their capacity. The bully uses sexual harassment to put the victim in his or her "proper place".

Besides these, social thinkers classified Sexual Harassers into some other types, i.e. serial harasser, pest, Intellectual seducer, Great Gallant, Incompetent harasser etc.

Ways to Stop Sexual Harassment

We have already mentioned about the effects of sexual harassment. It impacts on the human relationship which is most essential for an ordered society. Therefore, a fruitful attempt has been made by government to stop sexual harassment throughout the world. A good number of legal provisions are imposed by the governments in different countries. For example, The Anti-Sexual Harassment Act of 1995 (Philippines), The Discrimination Act of 1975 (United Kingdom), Criminal Code of Russian Federation, Code of Conduct for Gender Justice (Pakistan), Israeli Sexual Harassment Law of 1998, etc. Apart from these Legal provisions or Acts some of the ways are also suggested by sociologists to stop sexual harassment as mentioned below:

(a) A victim should face the harasser boldly. The harasser should be told about his offense.

(b) It should be disclosed to co-workers, friends, subordinates, relatives, policemen, concerned authorities etc., whom they trust. It should not be kept as secret. A victim should strive to find out if some others have also been harassed. Everybody as human being must offer their own help for possible collective action.

(c) Educational institutions should play an important role to stop sexual harassment. Moral teaching should be introduced as a compulsory curriculum by the concerned authorities in all educational institutions.

(d) Necessary agency should take complete responsibility for perfect socialization. People should be socialized perfect by agencies like family, school, and peer groups. Even adult socialization should be perfect which will be helpful for everybody to make awareness about morality and ethics in human society.

(e) Both formal and informal agent of social control should be more imposed and made more dynamic to stop sexual harassment. Social activists and other social organizations should take initiative to stop it. Women should be made aware about their right and proper justice.

It is also very interesting matter that though the sexual harassment is generally considered as morally deplorable behaviour, but it is not free from controversy. Accordingly, misunderstandings can abound. Moreover, sexual harassment law has been highly criticized by some of the prominent social thinkers. A section of feminist thinkers boldly criticize sexual harassment policy as helping maintain archaic stereotypes of women as delicate, sexual creatures. Who require special protection? Sexual harassment policies and legislations have been criticized as attempts to 'regulate romance' which goes against human urges. On the other hand, some other critics opine that sexual harassment is a serious problem, but existing views are not applicable in true. These views focus mostly on sexuality rather than on the type of conduct that undermines the ability of women or men to work together effectively. However, it is sure in Indian context that sexual harassment occurs as a result of an omission by the crisis in morality and ethics of the human beings, so, solution should be found to stop this type of problem from sociological viewpoint for the sake of a civilized human world.

Gender and Sexually Transmitted Diseases

Sexually Transmitted Diseases are most significant and burning problem which is concerned with public health. This problem is not only because of their severe complications and sequel, but also because they increase the risk for transmission of the human immunodeficiency virus. There is a strong connection between HIV infection and sexually transmitted diseases, especially those causing genital ulcers such as syphilis, cancroids, genital herpes etc. But Acquired Immune Deficiency Syndrome (AIDS) is most important and dangerous amongst all sexually transmitted diseases. It is recognized as a global problem. Now, number of AIDS patients has increased all-over the world. This disease continues to ravage families, communities and countries throughout the World. In India women account for around one million out of 2.5 million estimated number of people living with HIV/AIDS. Their heightened vulnerability has both socio-economic and biological reasons. Social scientists and social psychologists have already expressed that early marriage, violence and sexual abuse against women are the major socio-economic reasons for their vulnerability to HIV infection. So, it should be studied seriously from sociological viewpoint. The spread of HIV/AIDS poses a serious challenge to every nation across the globe. HIV/AIDS have the complete capacity to undermine the massive improvements that have been made in global health. Beside it HIV/AIDS make threat to worldwide overall development. Realizing the negative thrust of this serious situation. Former Hon'ble Prime Minister of our country Dr. Manmohan Singh has given a very significant statement that "HIV/AIDS has become a serious socio-economic and developmental concern. We have no choice but to act, and act with firmness, with urgency and with utmost seriousness..." Both male and female are affected by HIV/AIDS. Physiologically, young people are more vulnerable to STIs than adults; girls more than boys. Generally, it is noticed that most young people consisting of both male and female become sexually active during adolescence. Due to lack of proper guidance and information during this period they are more likely to have multi-partner unprotected sex with high risk behaviour groups. On the other hand, young women are biologically more vulnerable to HIV infection than young men. Social researchers have also proved by their studies that HIV/AIDS impact more on women. It is happened throughout the world. According to the report of the UNAIDS/WHO, in the sub-Saharan Africa, almost 57 per cent of adults living with HIV are girls and women.

Assam too is not free from affects of HIV/AIDS. The First HIV Positive case in Assam was reported in September, 1990. Assam stands as a very vulnerable state in India in terms of HIV/AIDS and the numbers of people infected by this disease is still increasing. Till 1st January, 2012, a total of 6,304 HIV/AIDS cases have been detected in Assam. But, a recently published technical report by NACO has estimates a total of 14,244 HIV Positive cases in Assam. This high rate of infection by this deadly virus in Assam has certain specific causes behind it. They are:

(i) High rate of illiteracy and ignorance towards Sexually Transmitted Diseases (STDs).
(ii) It is the gateway to the north-eastern states.
(iii) Large numbers of female migrants from other north-eastern states.
(iv) High prevalence of other Sexually Transmitted infection and risky sexual behaviour among young people.
(v) Existence of mobile and hidden nature of female sex workers, drug abuse, Injecting drugs, illegal drug trafficking etc.

Such factors are responsible for high number of HIV Positive people in Assam.

The report mentioned that in places where hetero-sexual contact is the principal mode of HIV transmission most of those affected are women. The effects of HIV/AIDS and concerned matters related to this disease should and must be discussed. Common question about HIV/AIDS is always raised that what is HIV or AIDS? In this context, following paragraphs are most important in this chapter.

HIV/AIDS – Basic Knowledge

AIDS stands Acquired Immune Deficiency Syndrome. Acquired means you can get infected with it; Immune means Immune, Deficiency means a weakness in the body's system that fights diseases and Syndrome means a group of health problems that make up a disease. This disease is caused by a virus HIV. HIV stands Human Immune Deficiency virus. Regarding its origin; still people are in confusion. Its origin is obscure. The virus is believed to have emerged as a result of a mutation of a monkey virus, as the AIDS virus and some simian viruses share some common viral protein antigens. The HIV virus attacks the T-Lymphocytes-T-in man, and as a result of destruction of these T-Lymphocytes, decreases the ability of the host to mount immune responses to infecting organisms. If anyone gets infected with HIV, his or her body will strive to fight the infection. It will make 'antibodies', special molecules to fight HIV. It destroys immune system of human being to a great extent. Because of AIDS, the body is not able to fight the diseases and becomes defenceless. The symptoms of opportunistic infection can be classified into four categories:

(a) Gastro-intestinal pattern.
(b) Central Nervous system.
(c) Pulmonary pattern.
(d) Fever of unknown aetiology.

AIDS infects white cells in the blood. It is also interesting that having HIV disease is not the same as having AIDS. Many people are HIV positive, but do not get sick for many years. As HIV disease continues, it slowly wears down the immune system. The early signs and symptoms of this disease are:

(a) Unexplained weight loss.
(b) Fever and night sweats and malaise.
(c) Swollen glands.
(d) Oral or Oesophageal candidiasis.
(e) Persistent watery diarrhoea.

It should be noted that having any of these signs and symptoms does not necessarily confirm the diagnosis of AIDS. They may occur in other diseases as well. The incubation period is the time between the entry of germs and appearance of symptoms and signs of the diseases.

Actually people do not get AIDS easily. He or she might get infected with HIV, and later he or she might develop AIDS. People can get infected with HIV from anyone who is infected. The blood, semen, vaginal fluid and breast milk of people infected with HIV has enough of the virus in it to infect other people. Generally, most people get the HIV virus by:

(a) Having sex with an infected person.
(b) Sharing contaminated needles.
(c) Being born when their mother is inflected.
(d) Multiple transfusions of blood or blood products.

The HIV does not spread easily. People cannot get it from coughing or sneezing, mosquito bites, sharing household items, or swimming in the same pool as someone with HIV. To infect someone, the virus has to get past the body's defences. These include skin and saliva. If skin is not broken or cut, it protects people against infection from sexual fluids or blood. HIV infection can occur during sexual activity. Sex is safe only if there is no HIV, no blood or sexual fluids, or no way for HIV to get into the body. Unsafe sex has high risk of spreading HIV. Experts of concerned subject have already expressed the 'Risk Chart' as mentioned below:

High Risk

1. Vaginal intercourse without a condom.
2. Anal intercourse without a condom.
3. Sharing needles, syringes and other body piercing instruments.

Low Risk

1. Oral sex.
2. Deep kissing.
3. Vaginal intercourse with a condom or female condom.
4. Anal intercourse with a condom.

No Risk

1. Touching-massage.
2. Masturbation-mutual masturbation.
3. Erotic massage—body rubbing.
4. Kissing.
5. Oral sex on a man with a condom.
6. Oral sex on women with a dental dam, glide dam, plastic wrap or cut-open condom.
7. Not sharing drug injecting, body piercing instruments, needles, syringes.
8. Using properly sterilized hospital tools.

In India, the first evidence of HIV was found in March, 1986 with Sera from 6 female prostitutes. At the beginning of 1986, despite over 20,000 reported AIDS cases throughout the world. At first, India had no reported cases of HIV or AIDS, but in course of time number of cases has been increased. In 1986, a very significant report was published, it stated:

> "Unlike the developed countries, India lacks the scientific laboratories, research facilities, equipment, and medical

> personnel to deal with an AIDS epidemic. In addition, factors such as cultural taboos against discussion of sexual practices, poor co-ordination between local health authorities and the communities, widespread poverty and malnutrition, and a lack of capacity to test and store blood would severely hinder the ability of the Government to control AIDS if the disease did become widespread."

Later in the year, HIV was found among sex workers, especially in Tamil Nadu and Chennai. Interestingly, it was transmitted to sex workers from foreign visitors. In this fact, a national AIDS Control Programme was also launched in 1987. This Programme involved with blood screening, surveillance and health education. By the end of 1987, out of 52,907 who had tested, around 135 people were found to be HIV positive and 14 had AIDS. Initially, these cases have basically occurred through heterosexual sex. But at the last of 1980s, a rapid spread of HIV was observed among injecting drug users. To observe it, India Government set-up the National AIDS Control Organization. It formulated the different policies to control HIV and AIDS. In the same year, the government also set-up state AIDS bodies in 25 states and 7 union territories. As per estimate of UNAIDS in 2006, there were 5.6 million people living with HIV in India, but the National AIDS control organization did not agree with UNAIDS. NACO claimed that the actual figure was lower. But it is sure that HIV was first found in Women's health.

Generally, it is noticed that AIDS patients or people living with HIV in India come from different socio-cultural background. The majority of infections occur through heterosexual sex. On the other hand, different studies have also shown that sexual activity between men is very common in India and because of unprotected sexual activity, people are affected by HIV. A large study in Andhra Pradesh found that 42 per cent of men who have sex with men in the sample were married, that had sexual relations with a woman within the past three months and that just under half had not used a condom. Therefore, awareness programmes should be promoted by governmental and non-governmental organizations amongst all sections of people. Treatment for people living with HIV is also very much essential in true sense. People living with HIV have faced violent attacks; reflected by families, spouses and communities; been refused medical treatment. But it is very unfortunate. While such strong reactions to HIV and AIDS exist, it is very difficult to make aware people about how they avoid this infection. So, no one should develop any negative attitude towards HIV and AIDS. Otherwise, many people having HIV will keep their status secret. They will have to feel that they should not talk about this. The discussion of HIV or AIDS should be opened. It is general problem for all. Commonly accepting that HIV only affects injecting drug users and gay men, but in large cases, women are highly inflected because their husbands have had multiple sexual partners.

AIDS now is recognized as a global problem. The number of AIDS patients has been increasing all-over the world since 1980. The disease continues to destruct families, communities and countries throughout the world. As per the records of WHO, more than 14,000 people become infected with HIV each day in the Third World countries like Bangladesh. Many behavioural and biomedical factors in the Third World countries are at the starting of HIV/AIDS epidemic threat. Infect all the components of the deadly triangle of AIDS-infection, malnutrition, and overpopulation are present here. Now, HIV/AIDS is not just concern for a particular country but also a social development issue closely linked to gender inequality, poverty, low levels of literacy and very poor knowledge about prevention throughout the world.

In Indian context, government and social activists take it as threat to new generation. The number of cases has been recorded by AIDS Control Broad in India. Apart from some other factors geographic situation of India is also one which is also seriously observed by the Indian Government and persons concerned with this problem. Now, serious epidemics are under way in several states of Indian sub-continent. According to India's National AIDS Control Organization, HIV/AIDs is not confined to vulnerable groups or to urban areas, but is gradually spreading into rural areas and the underpopulation. (NACO: 1999). On the other hand, young generation is now in big trouble because of HIV/AIDS. Even they are more likely to engage in high-risk behaviour such as unprotected sex with multiple partners. Generally, they have no information about the risks of infection and how to save themselves from it. Global estimates suggest that more than half of all new HIV infections occur among young people aged 15-24 (WHO: 2003). The sources of information and suggestion in reproductive health are rarely available in rural areas to the young generation. Although socio-cultural situations have been changing in

Rural India, but the mainstream attitude towards sexuality is still conservative. In different research works and empirical studies, it is noticed that many young people lack control over their sexual partner are, how many partners they have, or the circumstances and nature of sexuality. Lack of AIDS knowledge and lack of bargaining power of women with their sexual partner are also making them susceptible to the transmission of HIV/AIDS.

Divorce and Gender Exploitation

Divorce is also one of the concerned issues of present-day society which is result of domestic problem. Though, it is the turning away of partners from each other, it impacts on social relationship in broad sense. Divorces, which cannot be expressed easily, always get some unexpected problems. Legislations also permit divorce, but it will always have far reaching consequence in any human society. It is also true that there are different views and opinion regarding impact of divorce on society. J. Derrett and M. Duncan mention in their work "The death of Marriage Law" that divorce cases reflect a sick society, not a healthy one. Again Horton, Leslie and Paul opined that divorce and desertion are widely recognized as problems. They are not problems in all societies, as they do not exist in all societies. E.W. Burgess and H.J. Locke mention in "The Family" (1950) that "the most practical index of family disintegration for research purpose is divorce". E.R. Mowrer, an eminent social scientist has also mentioned that "family disintegration first impinges itself upon the attention of marriage relations expressed in divorce and desertion."[1]

Mobel Fonseca, who made a research on 'Marital Happiness' and discussed about divorce, remarked that "it can be safely asserted that separation, desertion and divorce as they represent various degrees of dissolution of the family are generally not favoured in Indian Society".[2]

Again at same time, social scientist like D.L. Sills opined that divorce is an imperfect index of marital disorganization, because, there may be disorganization without divorce. "It is also true that although many individuals regard state divorce as the only index of family disintegration, it is but one of the many signs, since, it represents the legal dissolution of the marriage, it certainly is final one".[3]

The word "divorce' is very significant from sociological view-point. It has relation with disintegration process of society. This word 'divorce' is a English term. It is derived from the Latin word 'divortium' which again is derived from 'dis' which means 'apart' and 'vertere' which means 'to turn'. It is the dissolution of the tie of marriage. Therefore, it is the turning away of partners from each other. It truly is a complete turn from the way of life the couple had so far.

In proper sense, Divorce means complete rupture of the marital relationship; the persons divorced returning to their original state of being free to marry. It is the legal ending of a marriage. It might appear as a simple phenomenon, but in practical life its implications are massive. According to *Encyclopaedia Britanica,* Vol. III (1910), divorce represents the end of that two people had for each other; it is the certificate that their relationship failed. According to the Hindu Marriage Act, 1955 (Amended up to 1976), "Any marriage solemnized, whether before or after the commencement of this Act, may, on a petition presented by either the husband or the wife, be dissolved by a decree of divorce."

We can try to be more conceptually clear the concept of divorce by getting proper understanding of three important terms, i.e., (a) separation, (b) desertion, and (c) annulment.

(a) *Separation:* Separation is a very initial informal step towards divorce. It is a temporary device to lessen the immediate conflict, or a legally recognized decision to live separately without divorcing. In marital separation, both husband and wife are discarded from normal marital association. It affects on their health, security and happiness.
(b) *Desertion:* Desertion is the irresponsible departure from the home on the part of either husband or wife, leaving the family to tend for it. It can be considered as an evasion of marital responsibilities and there is no way of ascertaining its true extent. S. Pothen has rightly observed in his work that, "A large share of desertion is never brought before any public agency. Many wives apparently feel the stigma of being abandoned and prefer not to report about their husbands."
(c) *Annulment*: Annulment is a court decision that the marriage contained some legal flow (coercion, fraud, unwillingness to consummate the union, monage, bigamy, etc.).[4]

It is a legal action that invalidates the marriage on the ground that it never legally existed and should not have occurred. It is a judicial declaration that no valid marriage ever existed between the parties in question.

Sociologists have been giving more emphasize on the study of divorce. Sociological study of divorce is most significant in India for certain important reasons. Eminent social thinker Promilla Kapur has mentioned that adjustment studies in India are very rare. "One of the probable explanations for the absence of these studies in India may be that social science studies as such started very late in the country, and have been focused mostly on the problems considered more important, that is, those which involve the majority of the population of the country".[5]

Mabel Fonseca also opined that study of interpersonal relationship in the family is lacking. Sociologists and social scientists were also appealed to study this problem in context of increased complex social settings. She remarked that increased complexities in the present social situation create new forces to interpersonal relationship in family is most important discourse for present-day situation. As a distinct field of sociology, the divorcers is a very vital content in the Sociology. On the other hand, divorce is one of the most striking themes of modern literature. It has drawn the attention of many social scientists during the last part of twentieth century.

So, study of divorce in India is most essential. Though, it is primarily a legal phenomenon, but this is very complex phenomenon and viewed from different aspects such as mental, physical, social and cultural. The law of divorce has made keeping in view all, or most of these aspects. The law of divorce has been made throughout the globe in which grounds are stipulated under which divorce may be availed of. These legal grounds are not just isolated legal causes, but they do signify the socio-cultural viewpoint also. So, sociological viewpoint is most significant to discuss about its root causes in true sense. H.M. Johnson, a sociologist who has expressed same important aspects of social and cultural structure which are likely to be concerned with a high divorce rate. He has categorically mentioned the following causes of high divorce rate:

(i) Religious tolerance of divorce
(ii) Legal tolerance of divorce
(iii) Increased industrialization

(iv) Urbanization
(v) Birth control
(vi) Greater geographical mobility
(vii) High vertical social mobility
(viii) Heterogeneity of population and high demands on the intimate affectional side of marriage (Johnson: 1961: 171-174).

All these causes are interdependent "From sociological perspective, causes are generally thought of as interrelated links in a sequential chain of events rather as single factors."[6]

Another eminent sociologist, Arnold W. Green mentioned in his book 'Sociology' that "the proximate reason for the high divorce rate is the prevalence of extravagant expectations in marriages, but the ultimate explanation is to be found in the social forces which undermined the traditional family's structure" (1964 : 437). William J. Goode also discussed different causes of divorce. He has summarized same variables with divorce proneness. These variables are: unhappy marriage life, urban background, marriage at very young age, short acquaintance before marriage, non-attendance at church or mixed faith, disapproval of the marriage by kin and friends, general dissimilarity in background, and variation in mutual role obligations of husband and wife (1963: 425). Another social scientist like Carter and Plateris also expressed that "a majority of divorces are obtained on grounds least unpleasant to advance under existing state law and easiest to establish in a legal proceedings".[7]

Divorce is viewed differently in different societies. In this writing, we are not to discuss about divorce in the Hindus, Christian, and Muslim etc. Here, we have to mention only some significant grounds of divorce which are laid down by Hindu Marriages Act (Section 13). These grounds are:

(i) Voluntary sexual intercourse with any person other than him or her spouse.
(ii) Cruel treatment.
(iii) Desertion for two years.
(iv) Ceasing to be a Hindu by conversion to another religion.
(v) Of incurably unsound mind /mental disorder.
(vi) Suffering from a virulent and incurable form of leprosy.
(vii) Suffering from venereal disease in a communicable form.

(viii) Renouncing the world entering any religious order.
(ix) Has not been heard of as being alive for a period of seven years or more.
(x) No resumption of cohabitation as between the parties to the marriage for a period of one year or upwards after the passing of a decree for Judicial separation.
(xi) No restitution of conjugal rights as between the parties to the marriage for a period of one year or upwards after the passing of a decree for restitution of conjugal rights.
(xii) Mutual consent, on the ground that they have been living separately for a period of one year or more, that they have not been able to live together, and that have mutually agreed that the marriages should be dissolved, on the motion of both the parties made not earlier than six months after the date of the presentation of the petition, and not later than 18 months.

Hindu Marriage Act [section 13 (B) amended up to 1976] has been approved divorce if both parties want divorce by mutual consent. According to this provision, both parties may jointly petition for a decree of divorce on three grounds:

(a) They have been living separately for one year or more;
(b) They have not been able to live together; and
(c) They have mutually agreed that the marriage should be dissolved.

It is also very interesting that for the purpose of divorce by mutual consent, the parties need not prove anything other than that is laid down in section 13 (B) as mentioned above. There are some extra grounds for a wife to present a petition for divorce. These grounds are:

(i) When her husband is guilty of rape, sodomy or bestiality;
(ii) When husband has married again; and
(iii) When her marriage (whether consummated or not) was solemnized before she attained the age of 15 years and she has repudiated the marriage before attaining the age of eighteen years.

Bigamy is also a most important ground of divorce. Bigamy means the crime of having two wives or two husbands at the same time. But in case of bigamy sufficient proof should be submitted. To bring home a charge of bigamy, it must be established that the alleged marriage had been solemnized after due observance of rites and ceremonies. Cohabitation with women for same time may not be taken as marriage, but continuous cohabitation for a number of years may raise the presumption of marriage" (Pothen 1986: 120). In this case only admission of allegation by the accused is not a sufficient proof, but following things are to be proved.

(i) That the complainant had been validly married the accused.
(ii) That the accused contacted a second marriage during.
(iii) Both marriages were valid and strictly according to law governing the parties (S. Pothen: 1987 : 120).

Domestic Violence against Women

Domestic violence against women is now a burning problem throughout the world. It is widely prevalent in both developed and underdeveloped society. It is considered as human right issue. Domestic violence seriously stands as a stumbling block for development. It is rooted in unequal power relations between men and women in society and can be understood within a gender framework.

Violence against women may occur in different forms. Generally, men have a tendency to dominate women. Men believe that they are physically stronger in terms of strength. They always feel an epic pride without proper rational thinking. So, they always feel superior than women. Releasing this very sorrowful tendency of male folk towards womenfolk, violence is considered as one of the significant contents of sociological discourses.

> "A narrow concept of violence may suggest an illegal act, criminal use of physical force, but it also includes exploitation, discrimination, upholding of an unequal economic and social status, the creation of an atmosphere of terror, a situation of threat, reprisal and other forms of political violence".[8]

The term 'Violence against Women' means any act of gender-based violence that results in, or is likely to result in, physical, sexual or psychological harm or suffering to women, including threats of such acts, coercion or arbitrary deprivation of liberty whether occurring in public or private life (Pyal & Diengdoh: 2009: 64). Generally, we have to find out physical, sexual and psychological violence in family. For instance: sexual abuse of female children in the household.

Domestic violence is related to exploitation. In behavioural terms, it can be considered as against women ranges from simple suppression to abuse, aggression, exploitation and severe oppression like wife-beating, rape etc. In general, it is a coercive mechanism to assert one's eagerness over another, in order to prove or feel sense of power.

From the close observation it is noticed that usually cases of domestic violence are connected with liquor consumption and extra-marital affairs of both husband and wife. In same case if the husband or wife has extra-marital relationship with opposite sex and it becomes open secret, then violence occurs in family life. After marriage no one can accept this type of relationship psychologically and because of it he or she usually develops the feeling of aggression in their mental set-up. As a result of this they become more and more violent in family life. On the other hand, liquor consumption also is one of the most important causes of domestic violence according to social scientists and psychologists. Gita Pyal and Donna R. Diengdoh also very rightly express their new opinion about liquor consumption and domestic violence in their article "Issue of Social Domestic Violence and Women Trafficking in Meghalaya" that "Men drink with callousness and gay abandon. The hard earned money of both the husband and wife is devoured by alcohol. Consequently, the wives resort to taking up extra jobs and hiding their income. Deaths due to the consumption of alcohol are increasing but there is no statistical data available." It is an observation in Meghalaya which is a hilly state of North-East India, but because of liquor consumption; there are lots of incidents taking place throughout the county, generally after consuming liquor husband stay in a widely excited and belligerent state of mind. He cannot understand the consequences of his actions. If husband takes so much alcohol; he assaults wife with full of excitement and his normal restraint is disappeared.

On the other hand, the liquor consumption cannot be considered as the main cause of domestic violence. There are many people who consume liquor yet they do not become violent. In this way, it is not clear whether liquor induces violent behaviour or whether it acts initially as a disinhibitor of pre-existing aggressive tendencies. Therefore, liquor consumption should be accepted as a cooperative cause rather than the main cause of domestic violence. Only one cause cannot be identified for domestic violence. Different forms of domestic violence are depicted with different causes and consequences.

Mainly wife battering is considered as one of the basic forms of domestic violence. It is a silent crime. Wife battering is now a global problem, but it is being depicted in different names. If it is accepted as marital problem, it would naturally imply that marital violence is highly directed by the husband against the wife and therefore, wife battering is more than any violence by wife against husband.

On the other hand, it is not a new phenomenon in our society. It is swept under for being 'too private' to be spoken or violence by husband against his wife is not new problem. "It is assumed by some to have begun with the first monogamous pairing. What is new, however, is that the fact that the public admission of violence against women occurs in a civilized society and the insistence by the government and responsible citizens that such violence is no longer acceptable, that we are therefore compelled to discuss the problem of such form of violence and search for solutions to alleviate it."

Interestingly, the common myth regarding wife battering is one that was part of the Napoleonic Code until a decade back. According to this code "Women like walnut trees must be beaten everyday." In European society, the people also believed that a man had right to beat his wife with a stick not thicker than his thumb. In Indian tradition, writings of Manu were also very pitiable towards womenfolk. Religion played very crucial role in reinforcing brutal attitudes to womenfolk. In fact over the ages religions have constantly admonished women to stay with her husband no matter how cruelly he treated her.

It is seriously noticed that maladjustment between husband and wife is commonly the cause of wife battering. It is the most prevalent form of violence against women. A who is battered is after given to understand that it is her fault but considering their activities or behaviours as fault depends on the attitude of men. In this way men behave aggressively and consider themselves as authority in the family. As per psychological interpretation also the causes of male violence apart is the involvement of men in retaining their power and authority in the family. "Far from being considered as grossly abnormal behaviour, the women they live with should preferably be viewed as an extreme form of normality, an exaggeration, in fact, of how society expects men to behave. So, only searching the causes of men violence towards women in society should not be encouraged from the 'activity assessment' by male counterpart." This factor of wife beating is more concerned with and more directly and undeniably related to the wider issue of power and inequality between the sexes than with the simpler issue of a husband indulging in violent/aggressive behaviour with Men having feelings of superiority complex use to behave aggressively in day to day life and the women live in a state of fear. Because of men's aggressive behaviour women bow down to men and start to look down upon herself and underestimates their value and efficiencies.

We generally feel that men tend to be more aggressive than women, but in some cases cannot be denied that women also are responsible for this problem. Some women are so haughty and intolerant and compel their husband's life so miserably through some unexpected behaviours. Due to certain misconducts most reasonable men also lose their control after a particular stage and beat-up the erring women.

Considering all phenomenon relating to wife-battering; sociologists came to consensus that it creates an undesirable situation in human society. It is also big threat to group life consisting of both male and female. It as a social problem breaks the social solidarity. Therefore, it should not be ignored by sociologists. In true, as like other public criminologists almost ignored wife battering as a problem until the 1970s. Just by the mid 1970s, wife battering was considered as prime issue by women's movement and brought it into public notice. During this period, a good number of social scientists and psychologists started to conduct some studies on wife battering as social and psychological problem. Murry A. Strauss found in his study that approximately 8.1 million USA wives are beaten by their husbands and one-fourth of all American couples engaged in at least one violent episode during their marriage. In India, Ram Ahuja dealt with an empirical study of 60 self-identified cases. He even pointed out some most important characteristics of wife battering in India as mentioned below:

(i) Wives under 25 years of age have higher victimization rates;

(ii) Wives younger to their husbands by more than five years run a greater risk of being battered by their husbands;
(iii) Low income women are more victimized though family income is more difficult to associate with victimization;
(iv) Family size and family composition have little correlation with wife-beating;
(v) Assaults by husbands generally do not involve severe injury;
(vi) The important cases of wife battering are sexual maladjustment, emotional disturbances, husband's inflated ego or inferiority complex, husband's alcoholism jealously a wife's passive timidity;
(vii) Exposure to violence of the assaulter in his childhood is an important factor in wife battering;
(viii) Though illiterate wives are more vulnerable to husband's beating than the educated wives, there is no significant relationship between beating and the educational level of the victims; and
(ix) Though wives with alcoholic husbands have higher rates of victimization, it has been observed that most of the husbands beat their wives not in a state of drunkenness, but while they are sober (Ahuja: 1992 : 218). Wife battering is the most under-reported crime in India.

Generally, women do not come forward to open their personal life. In most of the cases women enjoy the battering, but they never think to leave their husband and that is why this problem is not solved in proper sense. Even if a man is seen battering his wife no one dares to interfere because it is considered purely their family matter.

But, it is not right thinking of people in a civilized society. To eradicate the menace of rising domestic violence, public should take some responsibilities as member of human society. Today, besides wife-battering, violence against women is depicted directly in foeticides, female child killings, bride-burning, rape, eve-teasing, dowry death, witch-hunting, verbal abuses etc. In global level, United Nations has been striving to save women from any kind of violence. It has taken necessary action to promote gender equality since its inception. United Nations even established a commission on the status of women in 1946. At present it has five distinct bodies which deal with women's issues:

(a) The Commission of status of women and the Committee for

the Elimination of Discrimination Against Women (CEDAW).

(b) Intergovernmental Bodies.

(c) The Division for the Advancement of Women.

(d) The United Nations Development Fund for Women (UNIFEM).

(e) The International Research and Training Institute for Advancement of Women.

Most Interestingly United Nations has also adopted some most important conventions for giving equal status to women with men. In this context "Convention on the Elimination of All Forms of Discrimination Against Woman" is most significant which constitutes an international Bill of rights for women. It also sets up an agenda for national action to eradicate all discrimination in human society.

Again, The Vienna Accord, 1994 and the Beijing Platform of Action, 1995 and the Commission of Status of Women and the Committee for the Elimination of Discrimination Against Women are the main foundation of rights for women. It includes total 166 countries as member. But in true, though there are some important conventions and treaties, violence against women continues to be rampant in our society, "evidently, with a genuine intention to curb such violence, a Bill known as "The Protection from Domestic Violence Bill, 2002 has been introduced in the Lok Sabha on 8th March, 2002. This seem to be an appropriate step taken by the Government since section 498A of the India Penal Code has proved to be insufficient and as it does not cover a wide range of their offences" (Pathak: 2009:46). Therefore, these shortcomings should be carefully abolished for the proper implementation of a Bill to eliminate gender discrimination in proper sense. United Nations very sincerely set-up a legislation on domestic violence which states, "All acts of gender, based physical, physiological and abuse by family members against women in the family, ranging from a single assault to aggravated physical battery, kidnapping, threats, intimidation, coercion, stalking, humiliating verbal abuse, forcible or unlawful entry, arson, destruction of property, sexual violence, marital rape, dowry or related violence, female genital mutilation, violence related to exploitation through prostitution, violence against household workers and attempts to commit such acts shall be termed as 'domestic violence'."

Spousal Violence

The domination of man over women has strong historical roots. Early Roman law treated women as the property of their husbands, a custom reinforced by Biblical passages, Christianity, English common law and the more of American colonists (Dobash and Dobash: 1977: 178) women as property were subject to the control of their husbands or fathers who opted an authority of life and death over them. "Women have held no legal standing throughout most of history. Any harm committed against a woman was viewed as an offense against the father of husbands, not her consequently it was the male 'owner' who sought vengeance or compensation of his losses."[9] At the same time, a woman could not be an aggrieved party. The husband or the father was not held responsible for any injurious action by his woman. Buzawa and Buzawa (1990) observed very sincerely that "husbands or fathers were expected to punish women".[10] Even official punishment of women is also included as legal codes in many Western cultures. It is noticed that wife beating is very common phenomenon throughout the globe and it has a strong historical root. It is not a new phenomenon in our society. It is swept under for being 'too private' to be spoken or violence by husband against his wife is not new problem. People also realized it as one of the most serious problems in the mid of 1600 when Puritans and Massachusetts enacted laws against wife beating the family violence (Pleck: 1989). But this law was rarely enforced. During that time people believed that this laxity was due to the strong belief in family privacy and the acceptance of physical force by the husband as a valid form of discipline. The second stage was started in the late 1800s when some countries began passing laws restricting family violence. According to E. Pleck, "Worries over immigration raising crime, the use of alcohol and other factors promoted the passage of laws restricting family conflict and allowing for outside intervention".[11]

In some countries husbands were also flogged publicly as a punishment for beating their wives. The third stage was started in 1960s when general social unrest was depicted throughout the world and started to draw the attention towards demand for equality. Concerns over spouse abuse and family violence became rallying cries for the emerging women's movement. In addition social activists as well as some physicians raised voice against family violence and brought this problem to the attention of greater human society. In India, the evidences of the violence against women are also cleanly manifested in both the great epics *Mahabharata* and *Ramayana* where Draupadi was publicly tortured by the Kaurava and Sita was abducted by Ravana. Today, spousal violence, particularly violence against wife is depicted directly in different forms. Among these, wife-battering is a significant one. Like other Third World countries, women in India have been suffering by spousal violence in which wives are tortured and abducted by their husbands. Apart from this, the Indian women are naturally dominated by so-called patriarchal society. Even they have been compelled to believe that women are made the custodian of tradition that fixes her activities and behaviours by the society. But realizing this pliable plight of women folk, the campaign of movement to emancipate the women from inherent patriarchal taboos and norms was also started in India. In the mid of 1970s, a number of social organizations were emerged to protest any violence against women. As a result of these efforts, a good number of strict laws are enforced to eradicate the menace of raising spousal violence and other violence against women. But discussion about these laws and the way of its implementation is not an objective of this chapter. Here, looking to its objective theoretical interpretations of a spousal violence from sociological understanding is also incorporated.

It is also true that although there are several theoretical explanations about spousal violence, no clear and absolute consensus has been depicted as the causes of domestic violence. The theoretical arguments regarding spousal violence can be categorically classified into different categories. But in the context of spousal violence, especially, wife-battering, as one of the form of spousal violence, we may mention three important general theories, i.e. (i) Intra-individual theories, (ii) socio-cultural explanations (patriarchy), and (iii) the learned helplessness perspective.

The intra-individual approach strives to obtain an understanding of the offender's actions. It focuses on the question of what makes some individuals beat their wives, and addresses the psychological traits of women who tolerate violence. These theories locate the cause of deviant behaviour inside and individual. According to intra-individual approach, mental illness, stress, depression, low self-esteem, substance use, inter-generational transmission of abuse are often proposed as causes of spousal violence. The basic argument of this approach is that the offender, when striking out against his or her spouse, is venting frustration or anger at other people or things. The socio-cultural explanation considers abuse of women as an outcome of their historical treatment and the current patriarchal structure of society. Although people talk about an egalitarian human society irrespective of sex discrimination, however women in rural society are not on same strata with their male counterpart. Today's society remains predominantly patriarchal and that is why wife abuse or wife battering is largely ignored by the male dominated criminal justice system and society. In this context, it was also observed that Assam is also not free from male dominated practices at all and women have to go through men's will in every sphere. "Coupled with this view of a patriarchal social is the perception that violence is an integral part of modern society. It is socially accepted as a solution to problems."[12] The increasing number of personal crimes, especially among adolescents, is pointed to as evidence of this trend. "A world in which violence and aggression is an accepted means of dealing with disputes leads many feminists to conclude that male rely on violence to exert their position of power and to support the *status quo*."[13] Generally, in patriarchal society men carry an epic pride and consider themselves as superior than women. Due to this feeling, husband in some certain situations abuse their wives to prove themselves as superior in social set-up. Another most significant approach is the social learning approach: learned helplessness. Closely following the historical components of the socio-cultural explanations is the idea of learned helplessness. According to advocates of this approach, many battered women suffer from the syndrome she identifies as learned helplessness. The idea for learned helplessness centres upon three components, i.e. (i) information about what is going to happen; (ii) knowledge about, what will happen; and (iii) individual's behaviour towards the event that takes place. As stated by this approach, some women are unable to exert control over themselves or their environments. Women believe that they are helpless to alter their environment. In precise, they develop a belief that they are not in charge of the events around them and that they cannot change the flow of events. As a result, they become helpless in their struggle and may appear apathetic to some viewers. Battered women in spousal violence are also helpless because of their negative perception towards the incidents taking place in own family. As they belong to their husband for economic security, no effort is given by them to raise the voice against this abuse.

Realizing the gravity of this problem arising out of gender inequalities, many sociologists and social scientists have studied and analyzed it seriously. Krupp (2000) in his work expressed that spousal violence is unequally common and dangerous form of violence. There has been a recent surge in the development of risk assessment instrument in the field, but there exist few instruments to support efforts to formulate and manage risk and ultimately present spousal violence. Johnson and Nave (2002) in their research work "Spousal Violence in Bangladesh" explained spousal violence as a serious issue and also its impact on society. This violence refers to violence perpetuated by husbands. They studied physical violence in Rural Bangladesh in the decades of 1992, 2002. In 1992, Schuler found that 47 per cent women of lower socio-economic status in six villages in three districts of Bangladesh reported having experience of physically all abuse. They also explained that, the WHO (World Health Organization) study of 2001 found that 37 per cent of women in the urban study site and 50 per cent women in rural site reported having been sexually violated. Women who experienced spousal violence were 3.54 times more likely to have through of ending their lives. Both physical and psychological spousal violence contributed to contemplation of suicide by women. Srivastava (2008) in her work "Women and Crime" explained one of the gender related issue which is concerned with unwanted pregnancy. Even she focused on knowledge of women towards family planning to save their reproductive health. She observed clearly the hegemony of male in context of sexual activities. She mentions that sexual initiation is a traumatic occurrence accompanied by force and fear. It is also one kind of oppression of male in patriarchal society. At the same time, she also observed that apart from physical and sexual abuse some of the most intractable reproductive health issues of our time is unwanted pregnancy. The word marriage is as granting men right to unconditional sexual access to their wives. Women who lack sexual autonomy often the powerless to refuse unwanted sex or to use, thus are at risk of unwanted pregnancies. Gaylord (2005) one of the most prominent social scientists conducted a work on Battered wife and found that women who were seeking refuge from her husband's violence, they continuously assaulted and isolated from the family matters. He studied 22 years old women with a 31 old men with case

who has sexual intercourse with woman under circumstances falling under any of the following description: (a) Against her will, (b) without her consent, (c) with her consent, when her in fear of death or of hurt, (d) with her consent, when the man knows that he is not her husband, and that her consent is given because she believes that he is her lawful husband, (e) with or without her consent, when she is under sixteen years of age, (f) with her consent when at the time of giving such consent by reason of unsoundness of mind or intoxication, she is unable to understand the nature and consequence of that to which she gives consent.

From above description it is clear that women are the victim and men are the criminals. Traditionally, it was common belief that rape is an act carried out by men with sexual problems who are not able to control their sexual urges. Commonly, it is observed that men are supposed to have a virtually uncontrollable sexual urges which once awakened must find satisfaction unmindful of the consequence, and that is a purely sexual act engaged in for the purpose of sexual satisfaction. But interestingly the feminist thinkers have altered and developed a unique thinking for redressing the societal view of rape. They have reconceptualized this act and name it 'Violent crime' instead of 'sex-crime'. Carol Smart has viewed that rape is an act of extreme hostility and not a purely sexual act. According to Smart, it is a violent expression of hatred for women, not of sexual desire for them, though men achieve some kind of physical pleasure from raping women. But above all, generally a question has been raised in mind of us why a normal man wishes to secure sexual outlet by using his force? It is one of abnormal actions of human beings. June Hopkins, an eminent psychosocial thinker opines that rape is sexual expression of power and anger. It is motivated more by compensatory and retaliatory motives than sexual ones.

It is noticed that rape has been playing a very critical role in human society since perception. It is a conscious process of intimidation by which all men keep all women in a state of fear. J. L. Gupta mentions that "It is a symbolic means at some men's disposal of establishing power. The consequence of rape is so great that the victim will not reveal the event to others. Hence, it remains an under-reported incident".[15]

Indian is supposed to consider as modern society, but in true it is not correct. As India covers more rural areas, it is still traditional in nature. People of rural areas are being regulated and controlled by traditional norms and sanctions. So instance of incidence for rape is everywhere in India. Rape case is found throughout the ancient literatures. Compared to the Western countries; cases of rape are not more in India, but in course of time it is slightly increasing. Due to rapid growth of urbanization and industrialization, mind-set of Indian people is changed. They develop different types of attitude towards traditional norms in some ways, but women are not completely empowered. Their conditions are still not good. The conditions are so bad for a woman who reports rape and because of it, the victims will not reveal the fact in order to avoid the humiliation and shame that is poured on her by the society. On many situations raped woman is neglected and rejected by her own family and left to the mercy of pimps and prostitutes. Therefore, a good number of rape cases are not reported and kept away from public notice. Even they are compelled to hush up everything not to disclose about it. Sometimes, the raped woman commits suicide. The dead weight of religious and social values makes her an outcaste, an untouchable, a disgrace to her family unfit even again to live within the bonds of marriage. So, they are more anxious to maintain secrecy. Apart from these, a number of reasons compel the victims and their families to conceal the fact. The victims avoid attending identification parades for fear of retaliation by the suspect. Therefore, strong measures are necessary to prevent, physical and mental order of womenfolk in our society. In India, the Indian Penal Code (IPC) is the law of crime which has been playing necessary role to control and prevent rape. Of course, there is no any special provision in IPC. But in practice rape is considered as greater crime than other as per acceptance of IPC. Government is taking necessary action to stop this type of crime. But it is also true that whatever actions are taken still there are number of rape cases in India. It crosses all; racial, religious, ethical, age and socio-economic strata. So, unless there is no proper counselling among people it will be continued as a dangerous crime in society.

Social scientists as well as psychologists have been associating with the study of such dangerous crime. Psychologists Gebhard in his study mentioned that there are five categories of rapists:

(a) Moral delinquents, who use force to get what they want and commit, rape to satisfy sexual desire without taking interest in the victim. They are not hostile to females.

(b) Sadists, who have a strong hostility to females and get sexual satisfaction only when it is accompanied by physical violence.

(c) Explosives, who are normally 'upright' citizen. A disordered and disturbed family background usually underlies the behaviour of these offenders.

(d) Drunken Variety, who deludes themselves after drinking into thinking that a female is trying to seduce them.

(e) Double Standard, who divide females into 'good' and 'bad'. They rationalize the use of force, if necessary, on 'bad' girls.

From psychological perspective rapists are mentally disturbed person. They cannot control their mind. But social victimization and consequence of rape of sociological perspective is most significant. It is now identified as social problem. Rape is attributed to unhappy family life. Rape is a universal phenomenon which impacts on social relationship. Its aetiology is very complex and the manifestations are extremely varied according to time, place and person. In Indian context, sociologists find out some causes for which people commit such type of crime. There are:

(i) Disregard of moral values.
(ii) Lack of religious sanctions.
(iii) Pornographic literature and Blue Films.
(iv) Alcoholism.
(v) Broken home.
(vi) Lack of proper socialization.
(vii) Extreme social compulsion etc.

Apart from these sometimes crimes like rape occur due to some psychological factors. These are: (i) desire to rape, (ii) exhibition of potency, (iii) experience of pleasure in the pain of other (sadism), (iv) taking revenge on a woman etc. It should be mentioned that rape is an act of aggression and violence and it is committed by persons who are not motivated by sexuality rather, they are motivated primarily by power, hostility, and the urge to brutalize, humiliate and debase their victims.

Rape is a very serious problem for womenfolk. It is one instance where the atrocities of men against women become open. Rape is not the rape of women, but the rape of morality and the noble ideals of the society as a whole. Therefore, it should be stopped not only by law, but people should be educated and socialized to think in human society. In context of eradication of this type evil practice from human society, especially in India, different attempts have been taken in various ways. Movement of women's rights in India had also obtained a national character with an anti-rape movement in the beginning of Eighties. An anti-rape campaign was started throughout the country. It demanded some amendments in the Rape law. Even sizable lawyers raised the issue and wrote about this matter in some newspapers. On the other hand, some groups of dynamic and educated women also took up the issue as their campaign. They tried to draw the attention of the issue among the mass people. They ever collected signature a lot in support of their demands. They submitted memorandum to then Prime Minister of India for amendment of the rape law. Later on, other social organizations including some political parties raised the voice on this issue. But matter was not free from criticism. A serious debate on amendment of the rape-law was started in different regions of India. The proposed Rape Bill was the most controversial issue in the National Conference of Feminists which was held in Bombay in November, 1980. As a result of this debate amongst the feminist, it was resolved that demand of the women's organizations should be as follows:

1. A woman should be interrogated only at her dwelling place.
2. During interrogation by a police officer, a woman should be allowed to have a male relative or friend or women social worker present with her.
3. Women who are detained in custody should be kept in a separate lock-up meant for women only. If there is no lock-up available, the women should be kept in a child's or women's home meant for the protection and welfare of women.
4. The medical report of rape victim should state the reasons for arriving at the conclusions and should be forwarded without delay to the magistrate to avoid possibility of tempering.
5. During a trial of rape, the past sexual history of the rape victim should be excluded from the evidence.
6. A police officer who refuses to record a complaint should be guilty of an offence.

7. Section 375 of the Indian Penal Code which clarifies that the consent of the women in order to be considered as consent must be absolutely free and voluntary must be amended in view of the Mathura case (Mathura was a very teenage tribal girl who was raped by two policemen in the police station).
8. The provision about 'burden of proof' in section 111(a) of the Indian Evidence Act must be changed and it should be added that in cases where the accused in a rape trial is a public servant, police officer, superintendent or manager of a jail or hospital or remand home where sexual intercourse is proved and the woman makes a statement on oath that she did not consent to the sexual intercourse, then the court shall presume that she did not consent.[16]

As a result of this debate, the parliament passed a Bill which is commonly known as "The Criminal Law Amended Act (1983)". This particular Act amended the Indian Penal Code, the Indian Evidence Act and the code of criminal procedure with respect to the law connecting to rape. It also reveals the identity of a rape-victim is a serious offence. According to this Act, more or less some definition of rape is accepted of course, it provides some other new categories of offence of sexual intercourse by persons in custodial situation. The Act makes it clear that "Penetration is sufficient to constitute the sexual necessary to the offence of rape".[17]

As per section 376 of the Act, the minimum Punishment for rape is seven years and the maximum life imprisonment. But important matter is that people should not think to solve this type of problem through only legal provisions. In this regard, proper socialization is essential for all. Candidly speaking, women in our society have been considering women as Goddess or a housemaid or slave, but perhaps never a women or a companion. It is very pliable plight to womenfolk in India. Because of the possession of uterus by a female, she should not be considered as different from a male. In reality women and men are equal and their roles in life are very complementary. So, the enlightened males should take initiation for leading awareness campaign by which male in all strata of our society will respect the existence of women. Therefore, an anti-rape agitation should be emerged in the mind of male. The efforts of both male and female are most essential to eradicate the evil activities from human society. Social scientists, psychologists and scholars are generally responsible to emerge the concept of Gender differences. Really speaking this concept has existed as deception in the mental structure of men folk. They basically wish to opine on the basis of biological structure, which is not scientifically acceptable. But question is raised that is there any justification in considering a woman as physically weak? There may have the provision of division of labour in human society, but why the activities performed by women are underestimated solely for division of labour may be discussed. We should never consider the kitchen activities as the easiest one compared to the household activities inside and outside done by male. A women has a kind of physical power to be pregnant for producing child presently, some activities done by women have made the world astonished which are competent enough to prove their physical strength. On the wake of historic space expedition participated by a women like Kalpana Chawla. It cannot be said that women are physically and mentally weak. Marry Com and Kunjarani Devi, two athletes belonging to Manipur—a state of North-East India has shown brilliant performance in the field of sports and games having physical power, not only in National level, but also in international arena. Similarly, Mamoni Roysam Goswami, a Gyanpith Award winner, once in a public gathering acknowledged the importance of the physical power as like as intellectuality for creation of literary works. Of late, Rita Chaudhury, a highly acclaimed Assamese writer has also engaged herself taking much physical pain in possessing experience about a tribal community like Tiwa to make her great masterpiece 'Deo-Lunkhrui' for which she achieved most prestigious award of 'Sahitya Akademi', in 2008. Such type of evidence is available in present world. Thus, the concept of Gender difference is creation of our society. The male-dominant society has been exploiting women both physically and mentally by depriving their rights and dues throughout the ages. In our society, the women are thrown away as a particular weaker category by creating a concept like 'Gender identity' as male and female. This category is now especially discussed as Gender in academic discourses. A number of issues has arisen only for this particular category. These issues create some serious problems and break social equilibrium in true sense. So, it is necessary to study all the gender realized issue scientifically for the sake of our human society.

Female Foeticide

Violence against women is an age old phenomenon which has its genesis in the unequal gender relations between men and women in the society. Women have always been considered as weak, vulnerable, and in a position to be exploited. Gender violence depicts itself in various forms such as rape, wife battering, sexual abuse, marital rape, molestation, sexual harassment etc. One other very critical form of gender violence is female foeticide and infanticide. Killing of female child in the womb itself even before she is born is called female foeticide. Earlier it was not possible to determine the sex of the baby in the womb of the mother before delivery. But, with the advancement of medical science and technology, new techniques are devised for preventing the genetic, chromosomal disorders of the child in the womb. Now, it is possible to determine the sex of the child in the womb very soon after conception. This technique is known as 'amniocentesis'. Generally, this technology is applied to test the amniotic fluids, blood or any other tissues of a pregnant woman to identify the gender order. It is a harsh truth that even today, many parents in India wish to prevent the birth of a female child. The male child preference is so deep-rooted that people still fail to recognize the worth of a female child as the male is at the pinnacle of authority and power in our society. Along with other states of India, in Assam too female child has not received her due love and respect. Still, in certain areas of Assam, people believe that only a male child can be a '*bhetirokhiya*' which means the custodian of the family inheritance. Besides, a son only can give '*mukhagni*' to his parent's funeral pyre which will make the departed reach heaven. Again, only a son can provide security at old age, which a daughter is unable to offer as she will leave for her husband's family after marriage. This mindset makes the gender discrimination present in our society explicit.

In India men and women have equal status in the eyes of the law and female foeticide has always been considered as wrong and as a sin. Indian Penal Code provides penalties for aborting. Even a woman who causes harm to herself while aborting can also be punished under law. But in certain situations, right to abort has been conferred to the parents under "Medical Termination of Pregnancy Act, 1971" if it presents a risk to the life of the pregnant women. On the other hand,a Bill was formulated in 1988 which led to the "Legislation of Pre-natal

Diagnostics Techniques Act, 1994". But, this Act has been amended in 2003 and named as "The Pre-Conception and Pre-Natal Diagnostics Techniques Act, 2003". This Act has three important objectives which include: (i) prohibit sex selection before and after conception; (ii) Regulate Pre-Natal Diagnostics Techniques for the purpose of detecting genetic abnormalities or metabolic disorder; and (iii) Prevent their misuse for sex determination leading to female foeticide. However, only making laws to prevent such a hideous practice would not yield results until we can change our mindsets which put women in an inferior position and devalues her very existence.

Witch Hunting : A Societal Problem

The history of witch hunting is very important not only to understand it as a bizarre phenomenon, but also to understand the cultural diversities that exist across the world. The history of witch hunting dates back to several hundred years. During the period of fourteenth to seventeenth century, persecution of witches had led to the torture and murder of thousands of innocent women and men, even children. Naturally, there are many focal issues when it comes to the trend of witch hunting practices, but its history significantly has an influence from the belief in magic. The history of magic needs a greater note herein. The root of such witchcraft found existence from the religion of magic. The witch became expert in the magic and by exercising various magical devices. Witch hunts or the social process leading to it is one of the unresolved puzzles of pre-industrial history. It is understood that this witchcraft is also as old as ancient India. But so to say, there lacks a tendency for people of India as well as the people of other countries to write geography and history pertaining to witchcraft. Because of this there is no collection of facts pertaining to witchcraft. Some intellectuals opined that witchcraft is such a complex practice that it is hard to say something in right direction. However, certainly it can be said that witchcraft appeared from the beliefs, unbeliefs, thoughts and various superstitions. The so-called witch created disorder in the healthy environment. By virtue of this, the witch attracted people creating miracles. In this way, witchcraft developed in India from the ancient time and till now it influences uncounted men and women. Some of the intellectuals believe that witchcraft is nothing, but a superstitious belief. For fear of harmful effect, it is deeply rooted in the minds of people and bound to engage them in chaos. But they believed that the real existence of witchcraft in Indian society cannot be denied. Some of the logical minded men from Europe came in front to prove witchcraft useless and invalid saying that it is nothing, but hysteria and it did not influence Europe because of good healthy environment. But the fact is that witchcraft is not merely a superstition, but a culture throughout the past and is still alive significantly. The rites and rituals, customs and beliefs came to existence near about two to four thousand years ago in the heart of the people. The people observed keenly the inconsistence world and began to search the miracles. They try to understand the unseen from their logical end and control the strength of the unseen. By virtue of this, witchcraft is deeply rooted in civilization of India and regarded it as primitive science. The people who engaged themselves in witchcraft in ancient India can be said as first doctors or 'medicine man'. The materials they collected from various source of nature for treatment proved to be origin to invent medicines in modern science. In this context, it can be said that this medicine man was honoured as Doctor in the witch community in the Western country. The medicine man experimented with herbs, dried plants. This is the reason why the medicine man became herbal medicine user. The medicine man also keeps an eye over sun-moon-star and experiments about astronomical herbalist. He prepares some medicines and ointments from these herbs which are now well known in the modern medicine world. For example, Frond, poplar leaves, aconite, belladonna etc. The witch man prepared liquid medicine, or mixture from the flesh of animal. They also prepared medical ingredients which are intoxicating.

If we compare witch with priest, we see that the priest tried to control nature by worship and prayers to God, whereas the witch did it by some knowledge and devices. There is another logy like witchcraft which is known as sorcery. That is, the witchcraft is a bad craft; it only acted against the rule of God by virtue of spiritual things. Keeping in view of the object regarding witchcraft, we may say that magical spells and imprecations of witches and it is expected to later Vedic literature for which it became possible to write history regarding the impact of witchcraft in the life people of India. The potency of witchcraft as a phenomenon has drawn the attention of public, politicians and a variety of scholars in different fields of discipline from history to political science to medicine and from anthropology, sociology, religious science to language studies and literature. Thus, the effort to study the historiography of witchcraft is an interdisciplinary effort. People who supposedly had primitive minds strongly opposed the violations of the witchcraft accusations. Practically all individuals were afraid of harmful magic and were prone to superstition. The teachings of the church were a crucial factor behind such accusations. Another important factor which gained less concern and attention is the religious pragmatism and social life related to witchcraft and magic (Bhattacharjee: 2008). The church's creation of witchcraft and devil worship has exacted a heavy and bloody toll on humanity which still has not yet been fully paid themes such as ethnicity and colonialism in Europe were relevant to popular beliefs and to the way people dealt witch hunt. Witch hunts were thus not only a phenomenon of mass destruction, religious and social prejudices and backward mental status, in fact there were many other factors that contributed to the belief in witchcraft and witch hunts (Bhattacharjee: 2008).

Superstitions and superstitious beliefs are found all-over the globe. It is a universal phenomenon. Type and degree of beliefs may vary in different regions and cultures. Superstitious beliefs are the tendency to direct one's behaviour with irrational and mysterious fear or to gain privilege from the supernatural power. It is an irrational or non-scientific belief in the existence of certain powers operant in the world, with positive or ill (usually ill) effects. Superstitions generally refer to having belief that certain things and incidences have positive or negative implications. For instance, certain colour, day and numbers are perceived lucky or unlucky in some societies. In spite of science making great progress, the percentage of superstition is found to be increasing rather than decreasing. These beliefs impacts social lives of people by influencing their behaviour. Belief system is part of subjective culture that is usually imparted in human consciousness through mass media, cultural artifacts and educational institutions (Kelly and Ronan: 1987). Beliefs and attitudes are socially learned (Bord and Faulkner: 1975). Belief system as part of social structures has its own sociological implications. In spite of science making great progress, the percentage of superstition is found to be increasing rather than decreasing. Such a type of superstitious belief which goes to the extent of extreme form of violence that is murder is of 'Witch Hunting'. Witch Hunting is a social evil which is an intentionally behaviour to demean, dehumanize, harm, destroy, or kill innocent people.

A witch is a person with supernatural knowledge and powers, usually acquired from the Devil in exchange for her or his soul. Witches are believed to be able to change shape, transform others, cause of illness and death, concoct charms, and tell the future. Witch, can be of either sex (but in belief and practice more often female) who could mysteriously injure and kill people. Punishment of such people with supernatural powers is practiced in many countries across the globe and is significantly known as the practice of witch hunting. This superstitious practice leads to the persecution and death of hundreds of women and men every year. India, Kenya, Ghana, Nigeria, Somalia, Uganda, Papua Guinea, Saudi Arabia have thousands of such examples of the belief in witchcraft and which holds innumerable incidents of witch hunting. Premature deaths, unnatural death of people are often linked up with witch and their evil powers to destroy or bring destruction in the villages. Witchcraft narratives are evoked to manage such misfortunes—deaths, diseases and accidents.

The influence of witch hunting is plainly stamped on laws and morals, etiquettes and religion, technology and language. Witch hunts still occur today in societies where belief in magic is prevalent, from rural North India and from Papua New Guinea. Witch hunting is prevalent in many of the Indian states like Chhattisgarh, Assam, Orissa, West Bengal, Rajasthan, Andhra Pradesh and Maharashtra and some of the north-eastern states. Bihar alone accounts for a major chunk of witch hunting cases. The witch hunts in modern times are continuously reported by the UNHCR of the UNO as massive violation of human rights. Most affected by witch accusation are women and children and additional elder people and outsider groups of the community. Mainly the entire tribal belt of India suffers from the humiliation of this social evil. Acute poverty, little or no access to the most basic health care, education and sanitation are some of the factors leading to witch hunting. In these circumstances, superstition gains a force of its own. Bad crops, death in the family, loss of a child, persistent illness or drying up of wells or any such reason paves the way for this evil—problems are many, but the solution remains the same, locate the witch responsible for the problem and punish her. The method of treatment of the patients is also very much illogical. They normally go to the oracle, the person is locally known as the 'Bez' or a person supposed to have magical powers. He makes the people understand that the disease has been caused by some evil spirits controlled by a man or a woman. Such person under suspicion of witchcraft in this backward society is considered to be a bad sign for the people living in those remote areas who try to wreak harm upon him or her. The ongoing incidents are the result of this mentality. Moreover, many families were allegedly evacuated on various occasions by the enraged people on charges of practicing witchcraft.

Witch Hunting is a social evil, or is it? The studies about this practice depicts that for majority of them, it is not. While majority of them strongly believe in the practice of witchcraft, they are equally convinced that the practice of witch hunting is essentially for the benefit of the society (Saikia: 2012). That suggests that believe in witchcraft and fear of its potential to harm goes hand in hand. Such fear of the people towards the phenomenon of witchcraft which is fuelled by their undeterred belief in it stands as the pivotal cause for the heinous practice of witch hunting in different regions of the country. Even some studies reveal that fear is not always the spontaneous driving factor behind the practice of which hunting. Rather, it sometimes becomes a tool for this purpose. Property related issues and personal grudges are some of the very common reasons found in this research work which leads certain individuals to use fear as a tool to provoke masses towards witch hunting in order to satisfy their own personal vested interests. Thus, it has been found that the causes behind the practice may vary. However, with strong conviction it can also be said that no matter what the immediate cause of an incident of witch hunting; the fear of it remains a central issue. It is, hence, very important to examine why such beliefs and fear persist. The studies in India found that lack of education and poor health facilities play the role of major catalysts in this regard. The field of these studies exhibits very poor accessibility of education and health care facilities which contribute towards the practice of resorting to witchcraft in cases of illness and persistence of firm belief in it as education has a long way to go before it can contribute enough towards elimination of such beliefs among the people. People of same backward areas still consider lack of education and poor health care as the least important causes of witch hunting. However, it will be wrong to say that people are completely oblivious towards the fact that witch hunting is a very derogatory and evil practice. Under the influence of mass media and a rising voice in the society against the practice of witch hunting led by the intelligentsia and civil society groups people are becoming aware of the cons of such a practice. However, this awareness, at this point of time, is only capable of creating tiny ripples which are certainly not enough to shake the strong beliefs and perceptions which have been consolidated by culture and tradition over a long period of time. Hence, challenging such unshakable beliefs and eliminating them will be the key to the removal of the heinous practice of witch hunting in India.

Reproductive Health : A Issue of Gender Equity

The concept of Reproductive health is a state of complete physical, mental and social well-being and not merely the absence of disease or infirmity, in all matters relating to the reproductive system and to its functions and process (UN: 1990). The reproductive health is a very important aspect of women's health. However, such an important aspect is largely ignored in India. In rural India, talking about sex, reproductive problem is considered as the subject of taboo which results in a general lack of awareness among women regarding their reproductive issues. It is noticed that women have been suffering from different kind of diseases at their reproductive age. Reproductive health includes a satisfying and safe sex life which will be free from fear of disease. The ability of the reproductive and freedom to do so with the access to both infertility services and contraceptives is essential for ensuring reproductive choice for women and men. However, women are far from receiving such choice which makes them more prone to such diseases. The International Conference on population and development held in Cairo brought in the right to better sexual and reproductive health within the parameters of family planning. The Cairo conference provided a definition of reproductive health and it included sexual health which will enhance the life and personal relations of people and especially women (Saikia & Gogoi : 2014). Again this Conference also defined reproductive health care as the methods, techniques and services that contribute to reproductive health and well-being by preventing and solving reproductive health problems. The Cairo Conference also raised voice on women's empowerment and gender equality in context of sexuality and health. Therefore, the Cairo conference is considered as pioneer to bring forward a fully new approach to women's reproductive health. Reproductive health has been stated as "a state in which people have the ability to reproduce and regulate their fertility; women are able to go through pregnancy is successful in terms of maternal and infant survival and well-being; and couples are able to have sexual relations free of the fear of pregnancy and of contracting disease" (India's Family Welfare Programme: Towards a Reproductive and Child Health Approach, 1995, by World Bank). The history depicts that a new perspective on family planning was emerged in 1980. Showing reaction to the emphasis on 'overpopulation' and the projection of women as 'producers of too many babies', members of the International Women's Health Coalition highlighted on the tendency to neglect other aspects of women's reproductive health (Qadeer, Imrana: 1998). They opined that a reproductive health approach can make existing family planning and health programmes more strong and practical. Even, according to them, it can provide proper dignity and common rights to women. It was also expressed that ensuring the highest possible level of reproductive health care is fundamental to the exercise of her reproductive rights. Qadeer (1998) has rightly mentioned in this context that the concept now referred to a woman's capability to : (i) understand and enjoy her sexuality by gaining full knowledge of it; (ii) regulate her fertility through access to services and information; and (iii) remain free of reproductive morbidity (and death) and bear and raise healthy children. Therefore, knowledge of reproductive health for women is most essential to survive in a society. Now, Reproductive health is considered as a part of women's reproductive rights. Even Reproductive health is seen as a 'women's empowerment' and 'gender equity' issue. Many of women's reproductive health problems originate from gender inequalities and from the limited responsibility men take for the consequences of their sexuality and fertility (Ravindran: 1998). It this context, early marriage can be cited as a morbidity and mortality. T.K. Sundari Ravindran in *"Reclaiming the Reproductive Rights Agenda : A Feminist Perspective"* mentions that "unwanted pregnancies, back street abortions, and in most women are often the consequence of the male partners less than responsible burden of contraception in the vast majority of cases". Actually women need 'power' to control to enjoy good reproductive health. Correa and Petchesky (1994) also expressed that women need access to resource, like education and economic independence, household and community resources for basic infrastructural facilities. Therefore, these two important factors, i.e. 'power' and 'resources' are very significant for women's reproductive health. In light of this, reproductive health is not just a matter of preventing disease. Women's ability to bear children is strictly connected with the continuity of families, clans and social groups. From this point of view social scientists consider women's reproductive health as a issue of gender equality. Still in many areas of the world women have no adequate knowledge of the causes and consequences of their diseases. Even in certain condition, they are not aware of their health problem during pregnancy and childbirth. But reproduction is considered as one of the fundamental feature of all living creatures, in which, females play a vital role. Women are not only to reproduce the children, but also to ensure proper upbringing and socialization which makes good health of these women a prerequisite (Saikia & Gogoi: 2014).

Number of death cases among poor women due to reproductive causes has been hiking up throughout the world. As per report of the World Bank, about one third of the total disease burden among aged 15 to 44 years in the developing countries is linked to health problems associated with pregnancy, child birth, abortion, HIV, reproductive tract infections and among the diseases for which cost-effective interventions exist, reproductive health problems account for the majority of the disease burden in women of this age group (World Bank: 1993). Earlier reproductive health of women was not considered as most important matter in Assam. It was neglected for long time. Even, no special Programmeme had been implemented by State Government or any other non-governmental organization. But in course of time, matter of reproductive health in India became a serious issue of all. The focus on reproductive health has gained impetus because of new knowledge and deep understanding of women's health problems. In recent time; there is an increasing effort to consider women's health issue in a more holistic manner. It focuses on the health needs and concern of women in every aspect of their lives from birth to old age. A good number of Programmes have been introduced along with interventions to address women's health issues.

Notes

1. E.R. Mowrer (1942): *Disorganization – Personal and Social*, p. 474.
2. M. Fonseca (1996): *Counselling for Material Happiness*, Bombay, p. 21.
3. Marshall, Clinard (1965): *Sociology of Deviant Behaviour*, Holt Rinchart and Winston Inc., New York, p. 436.

4. William, J. Gorde (1963): *Family Disorganization in Contemporary Social Problems*, (ed.) Robert K. Merton & Robert A. Nisbet, London, p. 401.
5. S. Pothen, (1987): *Divorce: Its Causes and Consequences in Hindu Society*, Shakti Books, New Delhi, p. 10.
6. William M. Kephart (1977): *The Family Society and the Individual*, 4th ed. Houghton Mifflin Co., Boston, p. 517.
7. Carter & Plateris (1964): quoted by Winch and Goodman, in *Selected Studies in Marriage and Family*, p. 564.
8. Pathak, M. (2009): *Women Inroads*, Mittal Publications, New Delhi, p. 43.
9. Doerner, G. William & Lab, P. Steaven (1995): *Victomology*, Anderson Publishing Co., 2035, Reading Road.
10. *Ibid.*, p. 136.
11. *Ibid.*
12. *Ibid.*, p. 143.
13. *Ibid.*
14. Nehal, Ashraf (1997): *Crime Against Women*, Commonwealth Publishers, New Delhi, p. 17.
15. Gupta, J.L. (1980): *Challenge to the Fair Sex*, Gyan Books, New Delhi, p. 18.
16. Petel, Vibhuti (1984): *Needs and Rights: Experiences of Women's Movement in India*, United Nations University.
17. Flavia (1990): *Journey to Justice: Procedures to be followed in the Rape Case*, Majlis, Bombay.

12
Selected Case Studies

The book so far has shed light upon various issues and problems pertaining to women. A number of ideas, arguments, theories have sprung up through deep analysis of such issues and problems by various scholars which have also been covered in this book, although not exhaustively. However, the most important question remains; how do women deal with such issues and solve their problems. As far as I have observed, some women are not yet capable enough to challenge the problems they face with the strength and courage that is required. Because of the social compulsion, women even are bound to be under the constant control of men. The women are indeed socially captive. Even if the women understand their problems and realise that they have been subdued by their male counterparts in every aspect of their lives they are unable to resist this subjugation as they are always afraid of social customs and sanctions devoid of social security. Besides that, they are always under the shroud of shyness and hesitation. Thcir consciousness of their subjugation fails to convert into action in order to repel that subjugation. Some researchers have brought light on their emotion for which they become easily sentimental. In this context, following case studies are mentioned carefully which have been studies to understand the will-power and mind-set of womenfolk. The following case studies are more relevant:

Case Study-1

Name—M, 25 years old, having M. A. degree, stays in a semi-urban place. She considers herself free and frank, brave and mentally strong. But contrary to her those qualities, expressed by herself, she is not internally strong enough. She is ready to adopt herself in the materialistic society for attaining social security. This is a piece of conversation (on mobile phone) between the girl and her close male-friend at 11.30 p.m.

Friend—Hi, How are you? Are you ok? Missing you a lot tonight will you get trouble?

M—No, no ... nothing else. I too...

Friend—How are you spending your time?

M—Nothing, spending by eating; sleeping and getting reproach from dad.

Friend—Getting reproach from Dad? I cannot get...

M—Yes, dad pressurizes me to earn money. But how can I manage a job?

Friend—Oh! What are thinking now?

M—(Weeping) Thinking! Perhaps I might offer my body to someone else for .... From this particular case in Assam it is observed that the girl who thinks herself mentally strong, is also thinking to surrender herself instead of struggling bravely. It has shown that the women are responsible themselves in proving weak in our society.

Case Study-2

Name—B, 24 year old girl, Doing M.A. Programme in University stay in hostel. She talked with her close friend as follows:

B—I have no hope of living more.

Friend—Why?

B—I am exhausted.

Friend—Exhausted? Why?

B—Anubav (change the original name) has spoiled my life.

Friend—But you are a girl of strong mentality why... ?

B—He promised me to get married.

Friend—You gave all of you, as he had promised?

B—I dreamt to have a rich husband.

Friend—But said not to give importance on money...

B—These are only saying to others. Actually, I wish to be richer in my future ...!

This girl wants to pace as rapidly as her male fellows. But she has an ambition to be rich, for which she does not hesitate to violate all moral codes of the society.

Case Study-3

Name—L, 26 years, M.A. degree holders young girl. She is speaking sexual conversation with an elderly gentleman above 60 years. But she has no sexual urge or attraction to that gentleman. While asking her the reason behind this illicit action, she readily replies—"I am in want of a job". This gentleman who is powerful assured her to manage a job. This girl does not stop herself to be weak only for a job.

Case Study-4

Name—K, 26 years old girl, having Master Degree in Arts, who suffers inferiority complex and she is alienated from others. She is not economically sound. One day an educated gentleman has sexually abused her by seducing repeatedly. Which she was asked about this and her reaction, she only replied—"I do not repent for this..., I am not still hesitated to offer my body for getting money. It gives me pleasure too...".

It is also a kind of mental weakness on the part of the girl.

The case studies mentioned above prove that the women surrender themselves to the male, being mentally weak, for which they are solely responsible. Though, society is itself more responsible in emerging that kind of mentality in the mindset of the women folk. The attitude of a society is mainly influential force for these circumstances. Thus, it is necessary to study on social, cultural views of womenfolk. Women in true sense should change their mindset, if the women do not try to be stronger themselves, then gender discrimination as well as male-domination will continue forever. But it is also true that fifth generation women are enhancing their capabilities in all spheres. At last, it may be called that Life-style of present-day society has affected women's attitudes, thinking and beliefs. In this way, women should be more conscious for moulding a egalitarian and equilibrium society.

Bibliography

Abu-Habib, L. 1997: *Gender and Disability: Women's Experiences in the Middle East*, Oxfam: Oxford.

Afshar, H. 1991: "Women Development and Survival in the Third World," *Longman Perspective*, Vol. 49, London.

Agarwal, B. 1994: *A Field of One's Own*, Cambridge: Cambridge University Press.

Ahmed, L. 1992: *Women and Gender in Islam*, New Haven C.T. USA: Yale University Press.

Alison, M. 2007: *Women and Political Violence: Female Combatants in Ethno-National Conflict*, London: Routledge Publication.

Allen, B. 1996: *Rape Warfare : The Hidden Genocide in Bosnia, Herzegovina and Croatia*, Minneapolis: University of Minnesota Press.

Altekar, A.S. 1995: *The Position of Women in Hindu Civilization*, Varanasi: Motilal Banarsidass.

Baldick, R. 1965: *The Duel: A History of Dueling*, New York: Chapman and Hall.

Banerjee, S. 2005: *Make Me a Man: Masculinity, Hinduism and Nationalism*, New York: Sunny Press, Albany.

Baruah, S.L. 1992: *Status of Women in Assam*, New Delhi: Omsons Publications.

Boddy, J. 1989: *Wombs and Alien Spirits*, Madison: University of Wisconsin Press.

Butler, J. 2010: *Gender Trouble: Feminism and the Subversion of Identity*. New York: Routledge Publication.

Chakravarti, U. 2006 : *Gendering Caste: Through a Feminist Lens*. Kolkata: Stree Publication.

Chakrawarti, A. 1995: "Selective Readings of Feminist Scholarship", *Economic and Political Weekly*, Vol. 30, No. 27.

Channa, K. (Ed.). 1988: *Socialization, Education and Women Exploration in Gender Identity*, New Delhi: Orient Longman.

Channa, Karuna. 1990: *The Dialectics of Tradition and Modernity and Women's Education in India*, Vol. 39.

Chatterji, P. 1993: *The Nation and its Fragments.* Princeton: Princeton University Press.

Chodorow, Nancy J. 1989: *Feminism and Psychoanalytic Theory*, New Haven: Yale University Press.

Collins, P.H. 1989: "The Social Construction of Black Feminist Thought", *Signs Journal of Women in Culture and Society*, Vol. 14, No. 4.

Connell, R. W. 2002: *Gender.* Cambridge: Polity Press.

Cormack, M. 1961: *The Hindu Women.* Bombay: Asia Publishing House.

Datar, C. 2011: *Ecofeminism Revisited: Introduction to the Discourse*, Jaipur: Rawat Publications.

Desai, N. 1957: *Women in Modern India*, Bombay: Vora & Co.

Desouza, A. (Ed.). 1975: *Women in Contemporary India*, Delhi: Manohar Publication.

Devi, S. 1999: *Women's Status and Social Change*, Jaipur: Pointer Publisher.

Dube, S.C. 1963: Men's and Women's Role in India: A Sociological Review. Ward B. (Ed.). In *Women in New Asia : The Changing Social Roles of Men and Women in South and South East Asia*. Paris: UNESCO.

Dunphy, R. 2000: *Sexual Politics: An Introduction*, Edinburgh: Edinburgh University Press.

Eichler, M. 2006: "A Gendered Analysis of the Chechen War's," *International Feminist Journal of Politics,* Vol. 8.

Essed & Goldberg. 2009: *A Companion to Gender*, Blackwell: Kobayashi Publishing.

Evans, M. 2009: *Gender and Social Theory*, New Delhi: Rawat Publication.

Ferguson, K. E. 1993: *The Man Question: Vision of Subjectivity in Feminist Theory*. Berkeley: University of California Press.

Flavia, 1990: *Journey to Justice—Procedures to be Followed in Rape Case*, Majlis: Bombay.

Flax, J. 1987: "Postmodernism and Gender Relations in Feminist Theory", *Signs Journal of Women in Culture and Society*, Vol. 12.

Fonseca, M. 1966: *Counselling for Marital Happiness*, Bombay.

Foucault, M. 1981: *The History of Sexuality*. Vol. I: *An Introduction*, Harmondsworts: Penguine Publication.

Geetha, V. 2006: *Theorizing Feminism, 'Gender'*. New Delhi: Stree Publication.

Geetha, V. 2009: *Patriarchy*. Calcutta: Stree Publication.

Ghose, S.K. 1984: *Women in Changing Society,* New Delhi: Ashish Publishing House.

Godgi, D.R. 1965: *Women's in the Working Force in India*. Bombay: Asia Publishing House.

Gould & Kolb (Ed.) 1964 : *A Dictionary of the Social Sciences*.

Gupta, J.L. (Ed.) 1988: *Challenges to the Fair Sex—Indian Women, Problems, Plights and Progress*. New Delhi: Gyan Books.

Gupta, V.K. 2008: *Gender Discrimination and Human Right*, New Delhi: M.D. Publications Pvt. Ltd.

Hansen, L. 2001: "Gender, Nation, Rape: Bosnia and the Construction of Security", *International Feminist Journal of Politics*, Vols. 3, 4.

Hate, C.A. 1969: *Changing Status of Indian Women in Post-Independent India*, Bombay: Allied Publishing Pvt. Ltd.

Heidi, H. 1990: *The Unhappy Marriage of Marxism and Feminism: Towards a More Progressive Union*, Capital and Class.

Hirschmann, N. 2004: *The Subject of Liberty: Towards a Feminist Theory of Freedom*. Princeton: Princeton University Press.

Holt, P.N. 1969: *The Status of Women and Education in Rural Areas—A Sociological Study*. Madras: A.N.C. Publishing House.

Indra, M. A. 1955: *The Status of Women in Ancient India*. Banaras: Oriental Publishers.

Jacobs, S., R. Jacobson & J. Marchbank (Eds.) 2000: *States of Conflict: Gender, Violence and Resistance*, London: Zed Books Ltd.

Jacobson, D. & Waddleys, 1977: *Women in India – Two Perspectives*, New Delhi: Manohar Publishers and Distributors.

Jain, S. and S. Singal 1999: *The Gender Revolution: A Study of Educated Women*, New Delhi: Radha Publications.

Jones, A. (Ed.) 2004: *Gender and Genocide*, Nashville, Tamil Nadu: Vanderbilt University Press.

Kahn, P. 2004. "Rising Tide: Gender Equality and Cultural Change around the World", *Perspectives on Politics*, Vols. 2, 3 & 4.

Karlekar, M. (Ed.) 1995: *Search for Women's Voice*, New Delhi: Vishwa Prakashan.

Kumar, K. 2001: *Women and Civil War: Impact, Organization and Action*, Lynne Rienner: Boulder Co.

Kumba, M.B. 2003: *Gender and Social Movements*, New Delhi: Rawat Publications.

Lindsey, L. L. 2011: *Gender Roles: A Sociological Perspective*, New Delhi: PHI Learning Private Limited.

Maithreyi, K. (Ed.) 1986: *Women's Studies in India – Some Perspectives*, Bombay: Popular Prakashan.

Marshal, C. 1965: *Sociology of Deviant Behaviour*, New York: Half Rinchart and Winston Inc.

Mathews, J. 2003: *Women and War,* Ann Arboor: University of Michigan Press.

Mathur, D. 1992: *Women, Family and Work*, Jaipur: Rawat Publications.

Menon, N. 2012: *Seeing Like a Feminist*, Penguine Books.

Messner, M.A. 1997: *Politics of Masculinities, Men in Movements*. University of Southern California: Sage Publications.

Misra, G. & R. Chandiramani, 2005: *Sexuality, Gender and Right*, New Delhi: Sage Publications.

Mitchell, J. 1971: "Women: The Longest Revolution". In *Women's Estate*, New York: Pantheon Publication.

Mohanty, M. (Ed.) 2004 : *Class, Caste, Gender*, New Delhi: Sage Publications.

Mohanty, R.P. & D.N. Biswal, 2007: *Culture, Gender and Gender Discrimination,* New Delhi: Mittal Publication.

Mosse, G. 1985: *Nationalism and Sexuality*, Madision: University of Wisconsin Press.

Mukherji, I. 1972: *Social Status of North Indian Women*, Agra: Shivalal Agarwal & Co.

Nagich, S. 1997: *Status of Women in India,* New Delhi: Anmol Publications Pvt. Ltd.

Narasimhan, S. 1990: *SATI—A Study of Widow Burning in India*, Calcutta: Viking Publication.

Nehal, A. 1997: *Crime against Women*, New Delhi: Commonwealth Publishers.

Neuburge, L. & T. Valentini, 1996: *Women and Terrorism*, London: MacMillan.

Nongbri, T. 2003: *Development, Ethnicity and Gender*, Jaipur: Rawat Publications.

Pandey, S. 1994: *Women's Education and Development in Orissa: An Analysis, Social Changes*, Vol. 22.

Pathak, M. 2009: *Women Inroad: Path to the Twenty first Century*, New Delhi: Mittal Publication.

Patri, A. & A. Hans (Eds.) 2006: *Women, Disability and Identity*, New Delhi: Sage Publications.

Peteet, J. 1991: *Gender in Crisis : Women and Palestinian Resistance Movement*, New York: Columbia University Press.

Phillips, A. (Eds.) 1987: *Feminism and Equality*, New York: New York University Press.

Plumwood 1992: "Feminism and Ecofeminism", *Ecologist,* Vol. 22, No. 1, UK.

Poiten, G. & H. Rairkar 1993: *Indian Peasant Women Speak Up,* Hyderabad, Orient Longman Ltd.

Pothen, S. 1987: *Divorce: Its Causes and Consequences in Hindu Society*, New Delhi: Shakti Books.

Rai, B.C. 1989: *History of Indian Women and Problems*, Lucknow: Prakashan Kendra.

Ramachandran, V. 2009: *Gender and Women Development Issues*, New Delhi: Abhijeet Publications.

Rege, Sharmila (Ed.) 2003 : *Sociology of Gender*, New Delhi: Sage Publications.

Reiter, R.R.: The Traffic in Women, In *Anthropology of Women*, New York: Monthly Review Press.

Ruddick, S. 1989: *Maternal Thinking: Towards a Politics of Peace*, New York: Houghton-Mifflin.

Saha, C. 2003: *Gender Equity and Equality*, Jaipur: Rawat Publications.

Saikia, J. P. 2008: *Problems of Education and Rural Women*, Guwahati: D.V.S. Publishers.

Satchindanandan & R.P. Singha. 1984: *Women's Right: Myth and Reality*, Jaipur: Printwell.

Schneir, M. (Ed.) 1995: *The Vintage Book of Feminism*, New York: Vintage.

Scott, J. 1998: *Gender and the Politics of History*, New York: Columbia University Press.

Sharma, S.C. 1987: *Women and the Environment*, London: Zed Books Ltd.

Singh, S. 2009: *Feminism: Theory, Criticism and Analysis*. Delhi: Pencraft International.

Sjobery, L. 2006: *Gender, Justice and the Wars in Iraq : A Feminist Reformulation of Just War Theory*, Lexington Books, Lanham.

Walby, S. 1990: *Theorising Patriarchy*, Oxford: Basil Blackwell.

Weeks, J. 2012: *Sexuality*, London and New York: Routledge Publications.

William, J.G. (Ed.) 1963: *Family Disorganization in Contemporary Social Problems,* London.

Woodward, K. 2012: *The Short Guide to Gender*, New Delhi: Rawat Publications.

Index